TExES Elementary Sample Test Kit:

THEA
Pedagogy & Professional Responsibilities EC-4
Generalist EC-6

Teacher Certification Exam

By: Sharon Wynne, M.S.

XAMonline, INC.

Boston

Library of Congress Cataloging-in-Publication Data

Wynne, Sharon A.
    TExES Elementary Sample Test Kit: THEA, PPR EC-4 100, Generalist EC-6 191: Teacher Certification / Sharon A. Wynne. -1st ed.
    ISBN: 978-1-60787-306-8
    1. TExES Elementary Sample Test Kit: THEA, PPR EC-4 100, Generalist EC-6 191   2. Study Guides   3. TExES   4. Teachers' Certification & Licensure   5. Careers

Disclaimer:

The opinions expressed in this publication are the sole works of XAMonline and were created independently from the National Education Association, Educational Testing Service, or any State Department of Education, National Evaluation Systems or other testing affiliates.

Between the time of publication and printing, state specific standards as well as testing formats and website information may change that is not included in part or in whole within this product. Sample test questions are developed by XAMonline and reflect similar content as on real tests; however, they are not former tests. XAMonline assembles content that aligns with state standards but makes no claims nor guarantees teacher candidates a passing score. Numerical scores are determined by testing companies such as NES or ETS and then are compared with individual state standards. A passing score varies from state to state.

Printed in the United States of America   œ-1
TExES Elementary Sample Test Kit: THEA, PPR EC-4 100, Generalist EC-6 191
ISBN: 978-1-60787-306-8

TABLE OF CONTENTS

THEA TEXAS HIGHER EDUCATION ASSESSMENT

READING

Read the following paragraph, and answer the questions that follow.
This writer has often been asked to tutor hospitalized children with cystic fibrosis. While undergoing all the precautionary measures to see these children (i.e., scrubbing thoroughly and donning sterilized protective gear—for the children's protection), she has often wondered why their parents subject these children to the pressures of schooling and trying to catch up on what they have missed because of hospitalization, a normal part of cystic fibrosis patients' lives. These children undergo so many tortuous treatments a day that it seems cruel to expect them to learn as normal children do, especially with their life expectancies as short as they are.

1. **What is meant by the word "precautionary" in the second sentence?**
   (Easy)

   A. Careful
   B. Protective
   C. Medical
   D. Sterilizing

2. **What is the main idea of this passage?**
   (Average)

   A. There is a lot of preparation involved in visiting a patient of cystic fibrosis.
   B. Children with cystic fibrosis are incapable of living normal lives.
   C. Certain concessions should be made for children with cystic fibrosis.
   D. Children with cystic fibrosis die young.

3. **What is the author's purpose?**
   (Average)

   A. To inform
   B. To entertain
   C. To describe
   D. To narrate

4. **What is the author's tone?**
   (Rigorous)

   A. Sympathetic
   B. Cruel
   C. Disbelieving
   D. Cheerful

5. **What type of organizational pattern is the author using?**
   (Rigorous)

   A. Classification
   B. Explanation
   C. Compare and contrast
   D. Cause and effect

6. **How is the author so familiar with the procedures used when visiting a child with cystic fibrosis?**
    (Easy)

    A. She has read about it.
    B. She works in a hospital.
    C. She is the parent of one.
    D. She often tutors them.

7. **What kind of relationship is found within the last sentence that starts with "These children undergo..." and ends with "...as short as they are"?**
    (Rigorous)

    A. Addition
    B. Explanation
    C. Generalization
    D. Classification

8. **Does the author present an argument that is valid or invalid concerning the schooling of children with cystic fibrosis?**
    (Easy)

    A. Valid
    B. Invalid

9. **The author states that it is "cruel" to expect children with cystic fibrosis to learn as "normal" children do. Is this a fact or an opinion?**
    (Easy)

    A. Fact
    B. Opinion

10. **Is there evidence of bias in this paragraph?**
    (Rigorous)

    A. Yes
    B. No

Read the following passage, and answer the questions that follow.

Disciplinary practices have been found to affect diverse areas of child development such as moral values, obedience to authority, and performance at school. Even though the dictionary has a specific definition for the word "discipline," it is still open to interpretation by people of different cultures.

There are four types of disciplinary styles: assertion of power, withdrawal of love, reasoning, and permissiveness. Assertion of power involves the use of force to discourage unwanted behavior. Withdrawal of love involves making the love of a parent conditional on children's good behavior. Reasoning involves persuading children to behave one way rather than another. Permissiveness involves allowing children to do as they please and face the consequences of their actions.

11. **What is the meaning of the word "diverse" in the first sentence?**
(Average)

   A. Many
   B. Related to children
   C. Disciplinary
   D. More

12. **What is the main idea of this passage?**
(Easy)

   A. Different people have different ideas of what discipline is.
   B. Permissiveness is the most widely used disciplinary style.
   C. Most people agree on their definition of discipline.
   D. There are four disciplinary styles.

13. **Name the four types of disciplinary styles.**
(Easy)

   A. Reasoning, power assertion, morality, and permissiveness
   B. Morality, reasoning, permissiveness, and withdrawal of love
   C. Withdrawal of love, permissiveness, assertion of power, and reasoning
   D. Permissiveness, morality, reasoning, and power assertion

14. **What does the technique of reasoning involve?**
(Average)

   A. Persuading children to behave in a certain way
   B. Allowing a child to do as he or she pleases
   C. Using force to discourage unwanted behavior
   D. Making love conditional on good behavior

15. **What organizational structure is used in the first sentence of the second paragraph?**
(Rigorous)

A. Addition
B. Explanation
C. Definition
D. Simple listing

16. **What is the author's purpose in writing this?**
(Average)

A. To describe
B. To narrate
C. To entertain
D. To inform

17. **What is the author's tone?**
(Rigorous)

A. Disbelieving
B. Angry
C. Informative
D. Optimistic

18. **What is the overall organizational pattern of this passage?**
(Rigorous)

A. Generalization
B. Cause and effect
C. Addition
D. Summary

19. **From reading this passage we can conclude that**
(Average)

A. The author is a teacher.
B. The author has many children.
C. The author has written a book about discipline.
D. The author has done a lot of research on discipline.

20. **The author states that "assertion of power involves the use of force to discourage unwanted behavior." Is this a fact or an opinion?**
(Average)

A. Fact
B. Opinion

21. **Is this passage biased?**
(Rigorous)

A. Yes
B. No

Read the following passage, and answer the questions that follow.

One of the most difficult problems plaguing American education is the assessment of teachers. No one denies that teachers ought to be answerable for what they do, but what exactly does that mean? *The Oxford American Dictionary* defines accountability as the obligation to give a reckoning or explanation for one's actions.

Do students have to learn, for teaching to have taken place? Historically, teaching has not been defined in this restrictive manner; teachers were thought to be responsible for the quantity and quality of material covered and for the way in which it was presented. However, some definitions of teaching now imply that students must learn in order for teaching to have taken place.

As a teacher who tries my best to keep current on all the latest teaching strategies, I believe that those teachers who do not bother to read an educational journal every once in a while should be kept under close watch. There are many teachers out there who have been teaching for decades and refuse to change their ways, although research has proven that their methods are outdated and ineffective. There is no place in the profession of teaching for these types of individuals. It is time that the American educational system clean house, for the sake of our children.

22. **What is the meaning of the word "reckoning" in the third sentence?**
(Easy)

A. Thought
B. Answer
C. Obligation
D. Explanation

23. **What is meant by the word "plaguing" in the first sentence?**
(Average)

A. Causing problems
B. Causing illness
C. Causing anger
D. Causing failure

24. **Where does the author get her definition of "accountability?"**
(Average)

A. *Webster's Dictionary*
B. *Encyclopedia Britannica*
C. *Oxford Dictionary*
D. *World Book Encyclopedia*

25. **What is the main idea of the passage?**
(Average)

A. Teachers should not be answerable for what they do.
B. Teachers who do not do their job should be fired.
C. The author is a good teacher.
D. Assessment of teachers is a serious problem in society today.

26. **The author states that teacher assessment is a problem for**
(Average)

   A. Elementary schools
   B. Secondary schools
   C. American education
   D. Families

27. **What is the author's purpose in writing this?**
(Average)

   A. To entertain
   B. To narrate
   C. To describe
   D. To persuade

28. **The author's tone is one of**
(Rigorous)

   A. Disbelief
   B. Excitement
   C. Support
   D. Concern

29. **Is there evidence of bias in this passage?**
(Rigorous)

   A. Yes
   B. No

30. **What is the organizational pattern of the second paragraph?**
(Rigorous)

   A. Cause and effect
   B. Classification
   C. Addition
   D. Explanation

31. **From the passage, one can infer that**
(Average)

   A. The author considers himself or herself to be a good teacher.
   B. Poor teachers should be fired.
   C. Students have to learn for teaching to take place.
   D. The author will be fired.

32. **Is this a valid argument?**
(Easy)

   A. Yes
   B. No

33. **Teachers who do not keep current on educational trends should be fired. Is this a fact or an opinion?**
(Easy)

   A. Fact
   B. Opinion

34. **What is the best summary for the passage?**
(Average)

   A. Teachers need to be more accountable.
   B. Today's teachers must be responsible for student learning.
   C. Older teachers have no place in the classroom.
   D. Teachers are responsible for the quantity they teach, not the quality.

Read the following paragraph, and answer the questions that follow.
Mr. Smith gave instructions for the painting to be hung on the wall. And then it leaped forth before his eyes: the little cottages on the river, the white clouds floating over the valley, and the green of the towering mountain ranges which were seen in the distance. The painting was so vivid that it seemed almost real. Mr. Smith was now absolutely certain that the painting had been worth the money.

35. **What is the meaning of the word "vivid" in the third sentence?**
(Easy)

A. Lifelike
B. Dark
C. Expensive
D. Big

36. **What does the author mean by the expression "it leaped forth before his eyes"?**
(Average)

A. The painting fell off the wall.
B. The painting appeared so real it was almost three-dimensional.
C. The painting struck Mr. Smith in the face.
D. Mr. Smith was hallucinating.

37. **What is the main idea of this passage?**
(Average)

A. The painting that Mr. Smith purchased is expensive.
B. Mr. Smith purchased a painting.
C. Mr. Smith was pleased with the quality of the painting he had purchased.
D. The painting depicted cottages and valleys.

38. **The author's purpose is to**
(Average)

A. Inform
B. Entertain
C. Persuade
D. Narrate

39. **From the last sentence, one can infer that**
(Rigorous)

A. The painting was expensive.
B. The painting was cheap.
C. Mr. Smith was considering purchasing the painting.
D. Mr. Smith thought the painting was too expensive and decided not to purchase it.

40. **Is this passage biased?**
(Rigorous)

A. Yes
B. No

Answer Key

1.	B	21.	B	
2.	C	22.	D	
3.	C	23.	A	
4.	A	24.	C	
5.	B	25.	D	
6.	D	26.	C	
7.	B	27.	D	
8.	B	28.	D	
9.	B	29.	A	
10.	A	30.	D	
11.	A	31.	A	
12.	A	32.	B	
13.	C	33.	B	
14.	A	34.	B	
15.	D	35.	A	
16.	D	36.	B	
17.	C	37.	C	
18.	C	38.	D	
19.	D	39.	A	
20.	A	40.	B	

Rigor Table

Easy
1, 6, 8, 9, 12, 13, 22, 32, 33, 35

Average
2, 3, 11, 14, 16, 19, 20, 23, 24, 25, 26, 27, 31, 34, 36, 37, 38

Rigorous
4, 5, 7, 10, 15, 17, 18, 21, 28, 29, 30, 39, 40

READING RATIONALES

Read the following paragraph, and answer the questions that follow.
This writer has often been asked to tutor hospitalized children with cystic fibrosis. While undergoing all the precautionary measures to see these children (i.e., scrubbing thoroughly and donning sterilized protective gear—for the children's protection), she has often wondered why their parents subject these children to the pressures of schooling and trying to catch up on what they have missed because of hospitalization, a normal part of cystic fibrosis patients' lives. These children undergo so many tortuous treatments a day that it seems cruel to expect them to learn as normal children do, especially with their life expectancies as short as they are.

1. **What is meant by the word "precautionary" in the second sentence?**
   (Easy)

   A. Careful
   B. Protective
   C. Medical
   D. Sterilizing

Answer: B. Protective
The writer uses expressions such as "protective gear" and "child's protection" to emphasize this.

2. **What is the main idea of this passage?**
   (Average)

   A. There is a lot of preparation involved in visiting a patient of cystic fibrosis.
   B. Children with cystic fibrosis are incapable of living normal lives.
   C. Certain concessions should be made for children with cystic fibrosis.
   D. Children with cystic fibrosis die young.

Answer: C. Certain concessions should be made for children with cystic fibrosis
The author states that she wonders "why parents subject these children to the pressures of schooling," and that "it seems cruel to expect them to learn as normal children do." In making these statements, she appears to be expressing the belief that these children should not have to do what "normal" children do. They have enough to deal with—their illness itself.

3. **What is the author's purpose?**
   (Average)

   A. To inform
   B. To entertain
   C. To describe
   D. To narrate

Answer: C. To describe
The author is simply describing her experience in working with children with cystic fibrosis.

4. **What is the author's tone?**
   (Rigorous)

   A. Sympathetic
   B. Cruel
   C. Disbelieving
   D. Cheerful

Answer: A. Sympathetic
The author states that "it seems cruel to expect them to learn as normal children do," thereby indicating that she feels sorry for them.

5. **What type of organizational pattern is the author using?**
   (Rigorous)

   A. Classification
   B. Explanation
   C. Compare and contrast
   D. Cause and effect

Answer: B. Explanation
The author mentions tutoring children with cystic fibrosis in her opening sentence and goes on to "explain" some of these issues that are involved with her job.

6. **How is the author so familiar with the procedures used when visiting a child with cystic fibrosis?**
    (Easy)

    A. She has read about it.
    B. She works in a hospital.
    C. She is the parent of one.
    D. She often tutors them.

Answer: D. She often tutors them.
The writer states this fact in the opening sentence.

7. **What kind of relationship is found within the last sentence that starts with "These children undergo..." and ends with "...as short as they are"?**
    (Rigorous)

    A. Addition
    B. Explanation
    C. Generalization
    D. Classification

Answer: B. Explanation
In mentioning that their life expectancies are short, she is explaining by giving one reason why it is cruel to expect them to learn as normal children do.

8. **Does the author present an argument that is valid or invalid concerning the schooling of children with cystic fibrosis?**
    (Easy)

    A. Valid
    B. Invalid

Answer: B. Invalid
Even though to most readers, the writer's argument makes good sense, it is biased and lacks real evidence.

9. **The author states that it is "cruel" to expect children with cystic fibrosis to learn as "normal" children do. Is this a fact or an opinion?** *(Easy)*

   A. Fact
   B. Opinion

Answer: B. Opinion
The fact that she states that it "seems" cruel indicates that there is no evidence to support this belief.

10. **Is there evidence of bias in this paragraph?** *(Rigorous)*

    A. Yes
    B. No

Answer: A. Yes
The writer clearly feels sorry for these children and gears her writing in that direction.

Read the following passage, and answer the questions that follow.

Disciplinary practices have been found to affect diverse areas of child development such as moral values, obedience to authority, and performance at school. Even though the dictionary has a specific definition for the word "discipline," it is still open to interpretation by people of different cultures.

There are four types of disciplinary styles: assertion of power, withdrawal of love, reasoning, and permissiveness. Assertion of power involves the use of force to discourage unwanted behavior. Withdrawal of love involves making the love of a parent conditional on children's good behavior. Reasoning involves persuading children to behave one way rather than another. Permissiveness involves allowing children to do as they please and face the consequences of their actions.

11. **What is the meaning of the word "diverse" in the first sentence?**
(Average)

    A. Many
    B. Related to children
    C. Disciplinary
    D. More

Answer: A. Many
Any of the other choices would be redundant in this sentence.

12. **What is the main idea of this passage?**
(Easy)

    A. Different people have different ideas of what discipline is.
    B. Permissiveness is the most widely used disciplinary style.
    C. Most people agree on their definition of discipline.
    D. There are four disciplinary styles.

Answer: A. Different people have different ideas of what discipline is.
Choice C is not true; the opposite is stated in the passage. Choice B could be true, but we have no evidence of this. Choice D is just one of the many facts listed in the passage.

13. **Name the four types of disciplinary styles.**
    (Easy)

    A. Reasoning, power assertion, morality, and permissiveness
    B. Morality, reasoning, permissiveness, and withdrawal of love
    C. Withdrawal of love, permissiveness, assertion of power, and reasoning
    D. Permissiveness, morality, reasoning, and power assertion

Answer: C. Withdrawal of love, permissiveness, assertion of power, and reasoning
This is directly stated in the second paragraph.

14. **What does the technique of reasoning involve?**
    (Average)

    A. Persuading children to behave in a certain way
    B. Allowing a child to do as he or she pleases
    C. Using force to discourage unwanted behavior
    D. Making love conditional on good behavior

Answer: A. Persuading children to behave in a certain way
This fact is directly stated in the second paragraph.

15. **What organizational structure is used in the first sentence of the second paragraph?**
    (Rigorous)

    A. Addition
    B. Explanation
    C. Definition
    D. Simple listing

Answer: D. Simple listing
The author simply states the types of disciplinary styles.

16. **What is the author's purpose in writing this?**
    (Average)

    A. To describe
    B. To narrate
    C. To entertain
    D. To inform

Answer: D. To inform
The author is providing the reader with information about disciplinary practices.

17. **What is the author's tone?**
     (Rigorous)

    A. Disbelieving
    B. Angry
    C. Informative
    D. Optimistic

Answer: C. Informative
The author appears to simply be stating the facts.

18. **What is the overall organizational pattern of this passage?**
     (Rigorous)

    A. Generalization
    B. Cause and effect
    C. Addition
    D. Summary

Answer: C. Addition
The author has taken a subject, in this case discipline, and developed it point by point.

19. **From reading this passage we can conclude that**
     (Average)

    A. The author is a teacher.
    B. The author has many children.
    C. The author has written a book about discipline.
    D. The author has done a lot of research on discipline.

Answer: D. The author has done a lot of research on discipline.
Given all the facts mentioned in the passage, this is the only inference one can make.

20. **The author states that "assertion of power involves the use of force to discourage unwanted behavior." Is this a fact or an opinion?**
     (Average)

    A. Fact
    B. Opinion

Answer: A. Fact
The author appears to have done extensive research on this subject.

21. **Is this passage biased?**
     (Rigorous)

     A. Yes
     B. No

Answer: B. No
If the reader were so inclined, he could research discipline and find this information.

Read the following passage, and answer the questions that follow.
One of the most difficult problems plaguing American education is the assessment of teachers. No one denies that teachers ought to be answerable for what they do, but what exactly does that mean? *The Oxford American Dictionary* defines accountability as the obligation to give a reckoning or explanation for one's actions.

Do students have to learn, for teaching to have taken place? Historically, teaching has not been defined in this restrictive manner; teachers were thought to be responsible for the quantity and quality of material covered and for the way in which it was presented. However, some definitions of teaching now imply that students must learn in order for teaching to have taken place.

As a teacher who tries my best to keep current on all the latest teaching strategies, I believe that those teachers who do not bother to read an educational journal every once in a while should be kept under close watch. There are many teachers out there who have been teaching for decades and refuse to change their ways, although research has proven that their methods are outdated and ineffective. There is no place in the profession of teaching for these types of individuals. It is time that the American educational system clean house, for the sake of our children.

22. **What is the meaning of the word "reckoning" in the third sentence?**
     (Easy)

     A. Thought
     B. Answer
     C. Obligation
     D. Explanation

Answer: D. Explanation
The meaning of this word is directly stated in the same sentence.

23. **What is meant by the word "plaguing" in the first sentence?**
(Average)

    A. Causing problems
    B. Causing illness
    C. Causing anger
    D. Causing failure

Answer: A. Causing problems
The first paragraph makes this definition clear.

24. **Where does the author get her definition of "accountability?"**
(Average)

    A. *Webster's Dictionary*
    B. *Encyclopedia Britannica*
    C. *Oxford Dictionary*
    D. *World Book Encyclopedia*

Answer: C. *Oxford Dictionary*
This is directly stated in the third sentence of the first paragraph.

25. **What is the main idea of the passage?**
(Average)

    A. Teachers should not be answerable for what they do.
    B. Teachers who do not do their job should be fired.
    C. The author is a good teacher.
    D. Assessment of teachers is a serious problem in society today.

Answer: D. Assessment of teachers is a serious problem in society today.
Most of the passage is dedicated to elaborating on why teacher assessment is such a problem.

26. **The author states that teacher assessment is a problem for**
(Average)

    A. Elementary schools
    B. Secondary schools
    C. American education
    D. Families

Answer: C. American education
This fact is directly stated in the first paragraph.

27. **What is the author's purpose in writing this?**
    (Average)

    A. To entertain
    B. To narrate
    C. To describe
    D. To persuade

Answer: D. To persuade
The author does some describing, but the majority of her statements seemed geared towards convincing the reader that teachers who are lazy or who do not keep current should be fired.

28. **The author's tone is one of**
    (Rigorous)

    A. Disbelief
    B. Excitement
    C. Support
    D. Concern

Answer: D. Concern
The author appears concerned with the future of education.

29. **Is there evidence of bias in this passage?**
    (Rigorous)

    A. Yes
    B. No

Answer: A. Yes
The entire third paragraph is the author's opinion on the matter.

30. **What is the organizational pattern of the second paragraph?**
    (Rigorous)

    A. Cause and effect
    B. Classification
    C. Addition
    D. Explanation

Answer: D. Explanation
The author further explains what she meant by "...what exactly does that mean?" in the first paragraph.

31. From the passage, one can infer that
     (Average)

     A. The author considers himself or herself to be a good teacher.
     B. Poor teachers should be fired.
     C. Students have to learn for teaching to take place.
     D. The author will be fired.

Answer: A. The author considers himself or herself to be a good teacher.
The first sentence of the third paragraph alludes to this.

32. Is this a valid argument?
     (Easy)

     A. Yes
     B. No

Answer: B. No
In the third paragraph, the author appears to be resentful of lazy teachers.

33. Teachers who do not keep current on educational trends should be
     fired. Is this a fact or an opinion?
     (Easy)

     A. Fact
     B. Opinion

Answer: B. Opinion
There may be those who feel they can be good teachers by using old methods.

34. What is the best summary for the passage?
     (Average)

     A. Teachers need to be more accountable.
     B. Today's teachers must be responsible for student learning.
     C. Older teachers have no place in the classroom.
     D. Teachers are responsible for the quantity they teach, not the quality.

Answer: B. Today's teachers must be responsible for student learning.
The one idea that applies to the whole passage is Choice B.

Read the following paragraph, and answer the questions that follow.

Mr. Smith gave instructions for the painting to be hung on the wall. And then it leaped forth before his eyes: the little cottages on the river, the white clouds floating over the valley, and the green of the towering mountain ranges which were seen in the distance. The painting was so vivid that it seemed almost real. Mr. Smith was now absolutely certain that the painting had been worth the money.

35. **What is the meaning of the word "vivid" in the third sentence?**
    (Easy)

    A. Lifelike
    B. Dark
    C. Expensive
    D. Big

Answer: A. Lifelike
This is reinforced by the second half of the same sentence.

36. **What does the author mean by the expression "it leaped forth before his eyes"?**
    (Average)

    A. The painting fell off the wall.
    B. The painting appeared so real it was almost three-dimensional.
    C. The painting struck Mr. Smith in the face.
    D. Mr. Smith was hallucinating.

Answer: B. The painting appeared so real it was almost three-dimensional.
This is almost directly stated in the third sentence.

37. **What is the main idea of this passage?**
    (Average)

    A. The painting that Mr. Smith purchased is expensive.
    B. Mr. Smith purchased a painting.
    C. Mr. Smith was pleased with the quality of the painting he had purchased.
    D. The painting depicted cottages and valleys.

Answer: C. Mr. Smith was pleased with the quality of the painting he had purchased.
Every sentence in the paragraph alludes to this fact.

38. **The author's purpose is to**
(Average)

    A. Inform
    B. Entertain
    C. Persuade
    D. Narrate

Answer: D. Narrate
The author is simply narrating or telling the story of Mr. Smith and his painting.

39. **From the last sentence, one can infer that**
(Rigorous)

    A. The painting was expensive.
    B. The painting was cheap.
    C. Mr. Smith was considering purchasing the painting.
    D. Mr. Smith thought the painting was too expensive and decided not to purchase it.

Answer: A. The painting was expensive.
Choice B is incorrect because, had the painting been cheap, chances are that Mr. Smith would not have considered his purchase. Choices C and D are ruled out by the fact that the painting had already been purchased. The author makes this clear when she says, "...the painting had been worth the money."

40. **Is this passage biased?**
(Rigorous)

    A. Yes
    B. No

Answer: B. No
The author appears merely to be telling what happened when Mr. Smith had his new painting hung on the wall.

MATHEMATICS

1. $\left(\dfrac{-4}{9}\right) + \left(\dfrac{-7}{10}\right) =$

   (Rigorous)

   A. $\dfrac{23}{90}$

   B. $\dfrac{-23}{90}$

   C. $\dfrac{103}{90}$

   D. $\dfrac{-103}{90}$

2. $0.74 =$
   (Easy)

   A. $\dfrac{74}{100}$

   B. 7.4%

   C. $\dfrac{33}{50}$

   D. $\dfrac{74}{10}$

3. $-9\dfrac{1}{4}$ ☐ $-8\dfrac{2}{3}$

   (Average)

   A. $=$
   B. $<$
   C. $>$
   D. $\leq$

4. **303 is what percent of 600?**
   (Average)

   A. 0.505%
   B. 5.05%
   C. 505%
   D. 50.5%

5. **An item that sells for $375 is put on sale at $120. What is the percent of decrease?**
   (Average)

   A. 25%
   B. 28%
   C. 68%
   D. 34%

6. **Two mathematics classes have a total of 410 students. The 8:00 am class has 40 more than the 10:00 am class. How many students are in the 10:00 am class?**
   (Average)

   A. 123.3
   B. 370
   C. 185
   D. 330

7. **A restaurant employs 465 people. There are 280 waiters and 185 cooks. If 168 waiters and 85 cooks receive pay raises, what percent of the waiters will receive a pay raise?**
   (Average)

   A. 36.13%
   B. 60%
   C. 60.22%
   D. 40%

8. $\dfrac{7}{9}+\dfrac{1}{3}\div\dfrac{2}{3}=$
    (Average)

    A. $\dfrac{5}{3}$

    B. $\dfrac{3}{2}$

    C. 2

    D. $\dfrac{23}{18}$

9. Choose the statement that is true for all real numbers.
    (Rigorous)

    A. $a=0, b\neq 0$, then $\dfrac{b}{a}=$ undefined.

    B. $^-(a+(^-a))=2a$

    C. $2(ab)=^-(2a)b$

    D. $^-a(b+1)=ab-a$

10. The price of gas was $3.27 per gallon. Your tank holds 15 gallons of fuel. You are using two tanks a week. How much will you save weekly if the price of gas goes down to $2.30 per gallon?
    (Average)

    A. $26.00
    B. $29.00
    C. $15.00
    D. $17.00

11. In a sample of 40 full-time employees at a particular company, 35 were also holding down a part-time job requiring at least 10 hours/week. If this proportion holds for the entire company of 25000 employees, how many full-time employees at this company are actually holding down a part-time job of at least 10 hours per week?
    (Rigorous)

    A. 714
    B. 625
    C. 21,875
    D. 28,571

12. A sofa sells for $520. If the retailer makes a 30% profit, what was the wholesale price?
    (Average)

    A. $400
    B. $676
    C. $490
    D. $364

13. A car gets 25.36 miles per gallon. The car has been driven 83,310 miles. What is a reasonable estimate for the number of gallons of gas used?
    (Average)

    A. 2,087 gallons
    B. 3,000 gallons
    C. 1,800 gallons
    D. 164 gallons

14. **What unit of measurement could we use to report the distance traveled walking around a track?**
(Easy)

   A. degrees
   B. square meters
   C. kilometers
   D. cubic feet

15. **What unit of measurement would describe the spread of a forest fire in a unit time?**
(Average)

   A. 10 square yards per second
   B. 10 yards per minute
   C. 10 feet per hour
   D. 10 cubic feet per hour

16. **Express .0000456 in scientific notation.**
(Easy)

   A. $4.56x10^{-4}$
   B. $45.6x10^{-6}$
   C. $4.56x10^{-6}$
   D. $4.56x10^{-5}$

17. **A student organization is interested in determining how strong the support is among registered voters in the United States for the president's education plan. Which of the following procedures would be most appropriate for selecting a statistically unbiased sample?**
(Average)

   A. Having viewers call in to a nationally broad-cast talk show and give their opinions.
   B. Survey registered voters selected by blind drawing in the three largest states.
   C. Select regions of the country by blind drawing and then select people from the voter's registration list by blind drawing.
   D. Pass out survey forms at the front entrance of schools selected by blind drawing and ask people entering and exiting to fill them in.

18. The following chart shows the yearly average number of international tourists visiting Palm Beach for 1990-1994. How many more international tourists visited Palm Beach in 1994 than in 1991?
(Easy)

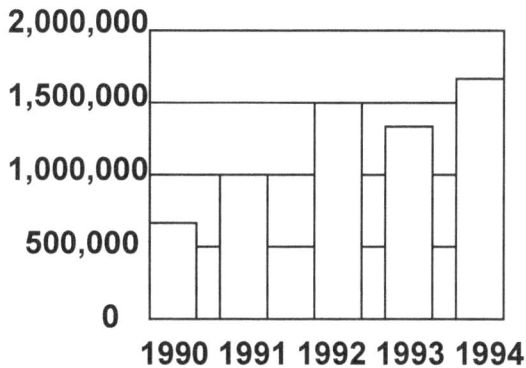

2,000,000

1,500,000

1,000,000

500,000

0

1990 1991 1992 1993 1994

A. 100,000
B. 600,000
C. 1,600,000
D. 8,000,000

19. Consider the graph of the distribution of the length of time it took individuals to complete an employment form.
(Average)

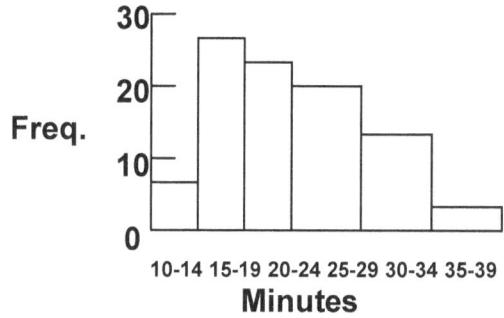

Freq.

30
20
10
0

10-14 15-19 20-24 25-29 30-34 35-39
Minutes

Approximately how many individuals took less than 15 minutes to complete the employment form?

A. 35
B. 28
C. 7
D. 4

20. Which statement is true about George's budget? *(Easy)*

   A. George spends the greatest portion of his income on food.
   B. George spends twice as much on utilities as he does on his mortgage.
   C. George spends twice as much on utilities as he does on food.
   D. George spends the same amount on food and utilities as he does on mortgage.

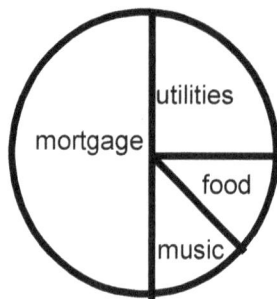

21. Corporate salaries are listed for several employees. Which is the best measure of central tendency? *(Average)*

   $24,000 $24,000 $26,000
   $28,000 $30,000 $120,000

   A. Mean
   B. Median
   C. Mode
   D. No difference

22. Compute the median for the following data set: *(Easy)*

   {12, 19, 13, 16, 17, 14}

   A. 14.5
   B. 15.17
   C. 15
   D. 16

23. State the domain of the function $f(x) = \dfrac{3x-6}{x^2-25}$ *(Rigorous)*

   A. $x \neq 2$
   B. $x \neq 5, -5$
   C. $x \neq 2, -2$
   D. $x \neq 5$

24. Which graph represents the equation of $y = x^2 + 3x$? *(Rigorous)*

A.   B.

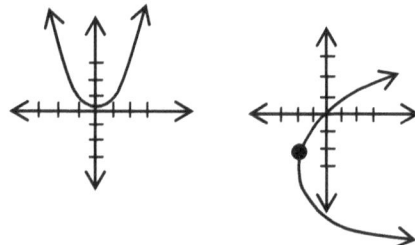

C.   D.

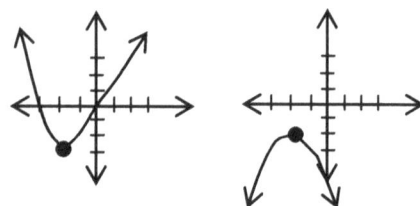

25. Choose the equation that is equivalent to the following:
(Rigorous)

$$\frac{3x}{5} - 5 = 5x$$

A. $3x - 25 = 25x$

B. $x - \frac{25}{3} = 25x$

C. $6x - 50 = 75x$

D. $x + 25 = 25x$

26. If $4x - (3 - x) = 7(x - 3) + 10$, then
(Rigorous)

A. $x = 8$
B. $x = -8$
C. $x = 4$
D. $x = -4$

27. Solve for x.
$$3x - \frac{2}{3} = \frac{5x}{2} + 2$$
(Rigorous)

A. $5\frac{1}{3}$

B. $\frac{17}{3}$

C. 2

D. $\frac{16}{2}$

28. Given the formula *d =rt*, (where *d* = distance, *r* =rate, and *t* =time), calculate the time required for a vehicle to travel 585 miles at a rate of 65 miles per hour.
(Average)

A. 8.5 hours
B. 6.5 hours
C. 9.5 hours
D. 9 hours

29. Solve the system of equations for x, y and z.
(Rigorous)

$$3x + 2y - z = 0$$
$$2x + 5y = 8z$$
$$x + 3y + 2z = 7$$

A. $(-1,\ 2,\ 1)$
B. $(1,\ 2,\ -1)$
C. $(-3,\ 4,\ -1)$
D. $(0,\ 1,\ 2)$

30. What is the equation that expresses the relationship between x and y in the table below?
(Average)

x	y
-2	4
-1	1
0	-2
1	-5
2	-8

A. y = -x – 2
B. y = -3x – 2
C. y = 3x – 2
D. $y = \frac{1}{3}x - 1$

31. Choose the expression that is not equivalent to 5x + 3y + 15z:
(Average)

A. 5(x + 3z) + 3y
B. 3(x + y + 5z)
C. 3y + 5(x + 3z)
D. 5x + 3(y + 5z)

32. Simplify: $\sqrt{27} + \sqrt{75}$
(Average)

A. $8\sqrt{3}$
B. 34
C. $34\sqrt{3}$
D. $15\sqrt{3}$

33. What is the equation of the graph below?
(Rigorous)

A. 2x + y = 2
B. 2x - y = -2
C. 2x - y = 2
D. 2x + y = -2

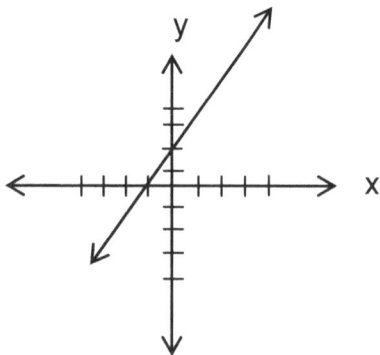

34. $f(x) = 3x - 2;\ f^{-1}(x) =$
(Rigorous)

A. $3x + 2$
B. $x / 6$
C. $2x - 3$
D. $(x + 2) / 3$

35. What is the area of a square whose side is 13 feet?
(Easy)

A. 169 feet
B. 169 square feet
C. 52 feet
D. 52 square feet

36. The trunk of a tree has a 2.1 meter radius. What is its circumference?
(Easy)

A. 2.1π square meters
B. 4.2π meters
C. $2.1\ \pi$ meters
D. 4.2π square meters

37. The figure below shows a running track and the shape of an inscribed rectangle with semicircles at each end.
(Rigorous)

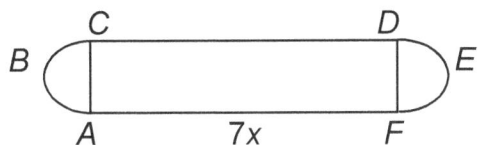

Calculate the distance around the track. (r = 1.5y)

A. $6\pi y + 14x$
B. $3\pi y + 7x$
C. $6\pi y + 7x$
D. $3\pi y + 14x$

38. What type of triangle is triangle ABC?
(Easy)

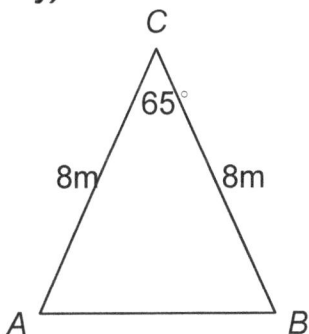

A. right
B. equilateral
C. scalene
D. isosceles

39. What is the area of this triangle?
(Easy)

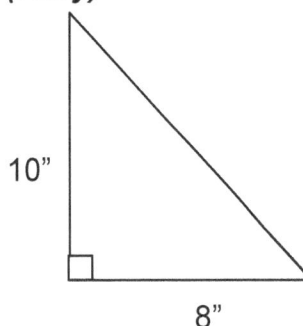

A. 80 square inches
B. 20 square inches
C. 40 square inches
D. 30 square inches

40. For the following statements
(Average)

I. All parallelograms are rectangles
II. Some rhombi are squares

A. Both statements are correct
B. Both statements are incorrect
C. Only II is correct
D. Only I is correct

41. Find the surface area of a box which is 3 feet wide, 5 feet tall, and 4 feet deep.
(Average)

A. 47 sq. ft.
B. 60 sq. ft.
C. 94 sq. ft
D. 188 sq. ft.

42. The owner of a rectangular piece of land 40 yards in length and 30 yards in width wants to divide it into two parts. She plans to join two opposite corners with a fence as shown in the diagram below. The cost of the fence will be approximately $25 per linear foot. What is the estimated cost for the fence needed by the owner?
(Rigorous)

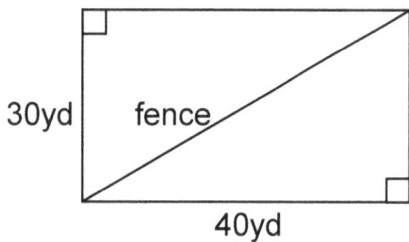

30yd | fence
40yd

A. $1,250
B. $62,500
C. $5,250
D. $3,750

43. Which term most accurately describes two coplanar lines without any common points?
(Average)

A. perpendicular
B. parallel
C. intersecting
D. skew

44. Set A, B, C, and U are related as shown in the diagram.
(Rigorous)

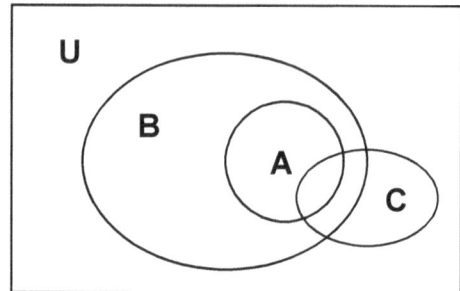

Which of the following is true, assuming not one of the six regions is empty?

A. Any element that is a member of set B is also a member of set A.
B. No element is a member of all three sets A, B, and C.
C. Any element that is a member of set U is also a member of set B.
D. None of the above statements is true.

45. **Select the statement that is the negation of the statement, "If the weather is cold, then the soccer game will be played."**
(Rigorous)

A. If the weather is not cold, then the soccer game will be played.
B. The weather is cold and the soccer game was not played.
C. If the soccer game is played, then the weather is not cold.
D. The weather is cold and the soccer game will be played.

46. **Select the statement below that is logically equivalent to "If Mary works late, then Bill will prepare lunch."**
(Rigorous)

A. Bill prepares lunch or Mary does not work late.
B. If Bill does not prepare lunch, then Mary did not work late.
C. If Bill prepares lunch, then Mary works late.
D. Mary does not work late or Bill prepares lunch.

47. **Select the rule of logical equivalence that directly (in one step) transforms the statement (i) into statement (ii),**
(Average)

i. Not all the students have books.
ii. Some students do not have books.

A. "If p, then q" is equivalent to "if not q, then b."
B. "Not all are p" is equivalent to "some are not p."
C. "Not q" is equivalent to "p."
D. "All are not p" is equivalent to "none are p"

48. **Given that:**

i. No athletes are weak.
ii. All football players are athletes.

Determine which conclusion can be logically deduced.
(Average)

A. Some football players are weak.
B. All football players are weak.
C. No football player is weak.
D. None of the above is true.

49. **Study the information given below. If a logical conclusion is given, select that conclusion.**
(Rigorous)

Bob eats donuts or he eats yogurt. If Bob eats yogurt, then he is healthy. If Bob is healthy, then he can run the marathon. Bob does not eat yogurt.

A. Bob does not eat donuts.
B. Bob is healthy.
C. If Bob runs the marathon then he eats yogurt.
D. None of the above is warranted.

50. **Given** $K(-4, y)$ **and** $M(2, -3)$ **with midpoint** $L(x, 1)$, **determine the values of** x **and** y.
(Rigorous)

A. $x = -1, y = 5$
B. $x = 3, y = 2$
C. $x = 5, y = -1$
D. $x = -1, y = -1$

Answer Key

1.	D		26.	C
2.	A		27.	A
3.	B		28.	D
4.	D		29.	A
5.	C		30.	B
6.	C		31.	B
7.	B		32.	A
8.	D		33.	B
9.	A		34.	D
10.	B		35.	B
11.	C		36.	B
12.	A		37.	D
13.	B		38.	D
14.	C		39.	C
15.	A		40.	C
16.	D		41.	C
17.	C		42.	D
18.	B		43.	B
19.	C		44.	D
20.	C		45.	B
21.	B		46.	B
22.	C		47.	B
23.	B		48.	C
24.	C		49.	D
25.	A		50.	A

Rigor Table

Easy
2, 14, 16, 18, 20, 22, 35, 36, 38, 39

Average
3, 4, 5, 6, 7, 8, 10, 12, 13, 15, 17, 19, 21, 28, 30, 31, 32, 40, 41, 43, 47, 48

Rigorous
1, 9, 11, 23, 24, 25, 26, 27, 29, 33, 34, 37, 42, 44, 45, 46, 49, 50

MATHEMATICS RATIONALES

1. $\left(\dfrac{-4}{9}\right)+\left(\dfrac{-7}{10}\right)=$

   (Rigorous)

   A. $\dfrac{23}{90}$

   B. $\dfrac{-23}{90}$

   C. $\dfrac{103}{90}$

   D. $\dfrac{-103}{90}$

Answer: D. $\dfrac{-103}{90}$

Find the LCD of $\dfrac{-4}{9}$ and $\dfrac{-7}{10}$. The LCD is 90, so you get $\dfrac{-40}{90}+\dfrac{-63}{90}=\dfrac{-103}{90}$

2. **0.74 =**
   (Easy)

   A. $\dfrac{74}{100}$

   B. 7.4%

   C. $\dfrac{33}{50}$

   D. $\dfrac{74}{10}$

Answer: A. $\dfrac{74}{100}$

0.74Ⓧ the 4 is in the hundredths place, so the answer is $\dfrac{74}{100}$

3. $-9\dfrac{1}{4}$ ☐ $-8\dfrac{2}{3}$

    (Average)

    A. $=$
    B. $<$
    C. $>$
    D. $\leq$

Answer: B. $<$

The larger the absolute value of a negative number, the smaller the negative number is. The absolute value of $-9\dfrac{1}{4}$ is $9\dfrac{1}{4}$ which is larger than the absolute value of $-8\dfrac{2}{3}$, which is $8\dfrac{2}{3}$. Therefore, the relationship should be $-9\dfrac{1}{4} < -8\dfrac{2}{3}$

4.   **303 is what percent of 600?**
    (Average)

    A. 0.505%
    B. 5.05%
    C. 505%
    D. 50.5%

Answer: D. 50.5%

Use x for the percent. $600x = 303$. $\dfrac{600x}{600} = \dfrac{303}{600} \rightarrow x = 0.505 = 50.5\%$

5.   **An item that sells for \$375 is put on sale at \$120. What is the percent of decrease?**
    (Average)

    A. 25%
    B. 28%
    C. 68%
    D. 34%

Answer: C. 68%

Use $(1 - x)$ as the discount. $375x = 120$.
$375(1 - x) = 120 \rightarrow 375 - 375x = 120 \rightarrow 375x = 255 \rightarrow x = 0.68 = 68\%$

6. **Two mathematics classes have a total of 410 students. The 8:00 am class has 40 more than the 10:00 am class. How many students are in the 10:00 am class?**
    (Average)

    A. 123.3
    B. 370
    C. 185
    D. 330

Answer: C. 185
Let x = # of students in the 8 am class and $x - 40$ = # of students in the 10 am class. $x + (x - 40) = 410 \rightarrow 2x - 40 = 410 \rightarrow 2x = 450 \rightarrow x = 225$. So there are 225 students in the 8 am class, and $225 - 40 = 185$ in the 10 am class.

7. **A restaurant employs 465 people. There are 280 waiters and 185 cooks. If 168 waiters and 85 cooks receive pay raises, what percent of the waiters will receive a pay raise?**
    (Average)

    A. 36.13%
    B. 60%
    C. 60.22%
    D. 40%

Answer: B. 60%
The total number of waiters is 280 and only 168 of them get a pay raise. Divide the number getting a raise by the total number of waiters to get the percent. $\dfrac{168}{280} = 0.6 = 60\%$

8. $\dfrac{7}{9} + \dfrac{1}{3} \div \dfrac{2}{3} =$

   (Average)

   A. $\dfrac{5}{3}$

   B. $\dfrac{3}{2}$

   C. 2

   D. $\dfrac{23}{18}$

Answer: D. $\dfrac{23}{18}$

First, do the division.

$\dfrac{1}{3} \div \dfrac{2}{3} = \dfrac{1}{3} \times \dfrac{3}{2} = \dfrac{1}{2}$

Add.

$\dfrac{7}{9} + \dfrac{1}{2} = \dfrac{14}{18} + \dfrac{9}{18} = \dfrac{23}{18}$

9. **Choose the statement that is true for all real numbers.**
   (Rigorous)

   A. $a = 0, b \neq 0$, then $\dfrac{b}{a}$ = undefined.

   B. $^-(a + (^-a)) = 2a$

   C. $2(ab) = ^-(2a)b$

   D. $^-a(b + 1) = ab - a$

Answer: A. $a = 0, b \neq 0$, then $\dfrac{b}{a}$ = undefined.

A is the correct answer because any number divided by 0 is undefined.

10. The price of gas was $3.27 per gallon. Your tank holds 15 gallons of fuel. You are using two tanks a week. How much will you save weekly if the price of gas goes down to $2.30 per gallon? *(Average)*

A. $26.00
B. $29.00
C. $15.00
D. $17.00

Answer: B. $29.00
15 gallons x 2 tanks = 30 gallons a week
= 30 gallons x $3.27 = $98.10
30 gallons x $2.30 = $69.00
$98.10 - $69.00 = $29.10 is approximately $29.00.

11. In a sample of 40 full-time employees at a particular company, 35 were also holding down a part-time job requiring at least 10 hours/week. If this proportion holds for the entire company of 25000 employees, how many full-time employees at this company are actually holding down a part-time job of at least 10 hours per week? *(Rigorous)*

A. 714
B. 625
C. 21,875
D. 28,571

Answer: C. 21, 875
$\frac{35}{40}$ full time employees have a part time job also. Out of 25,000 full time employees, the number that also have a part time job is

$\frac{35}{40} = \frac{x}{25000} \rightarrow 40x = 875000 \rightarrow x = 21875$, so 2,1875 full time employees also have a part time job.

12. **A sofa sells for $520. If the retailer makes a 30% profit, what was the wholesale price?**
(Average)

   A. $400
   B. $676
   C. $490
   D. $364

Answer: A. $400
$400; Let x be the wholesale price, then x + .30x = 520, 1.30x = 520. divide both sides by 1.30.

13. **A car gets 25.36 miles per gallon. The car has been driven 83,310 miles. What is a reasonable estimate for the number of gallons of gas used?**
(Average)

   A. 2,087 gallons
   B. 3,000 gallons
   C. 1,800 gallons
   D. 164 gallons

Answer: B. 3,000 gallons
Divide the number of miles by the miles per gallon to determine the approximate number of gallons of gas used. $\dfrac{83310 \text{ miles}}{25.36 \text{ miles per gallon}} = 3285$ gallons. This is approximately 3000 gallons.

14. **What unit of measurement could we use to report the distance traveled walking around a track?**
(Easy)

   A. degrees
   B. square meters
   C. kilometers
   D. cubic feet

Answer: C. kilometers
Degrees measures angles, square meters measures area, cubic feet measure volume, and kilometers measures length. Kilometers is the only reasonable answer.

15. **What unit of measurement would describe the spread of a forest fire in a unit time?**
(Average)

    A. 10 square yards per second
    B. 10 yards per minute
    C. 10 feet per hour
    D. 10 cubic feet per hour

Answer: A. 10 square yards per second
The only appropriate answer is one that describes "an area" of forest consumed per unit time. All answers are not units of area measurement except answer A.

16. **Express .0000456 in scientific notation.**
(Easy)

    A. $4.56x10^{-4}$
    B. $45.6x10^{-6}$
    C. $4.56x10^{-6}$
    D. $4.56x10^{-5}$

Answer: D. $4.56x10^{-5}$
In scientific notation, the decimal point belongs to the right of the 4, the first significant digit. To get from 4.56 x 10^{-5} back to 0.0000456, we would move the decimal point 5 places to the left.

17. **A student organization is interested in determining how strong the support is among registered voters in the United States for the president's education plan. Which of the following procedures would be most appropriate for selecting a statistically unbiased sample?**
(Average)

    A. Having viewers call in to a nationally broad-cast talk show and give their opinions.
    B. Survey registered voters selected by blind drawing in the three largest states.
    C. Select regions of the country by blind drawing and then select people from the voter's registration list by blind drawing.
    D. Pass out survey forms at the front entrance of schools selected by blind drawing and ask people entering and exiting to fill them in.

Answer: C. Select regions of the country by blind drawing and then select people from the voter's registration list by blind drawing.
C is the best answer because it is random and it surveys a larger population.

18. The following chart shows the yearly average number of international tourists visiting Palm Beach for 1990-1994. How many more international tourists visited Palm Beach in 1994 than in 1991? *(Easy)*

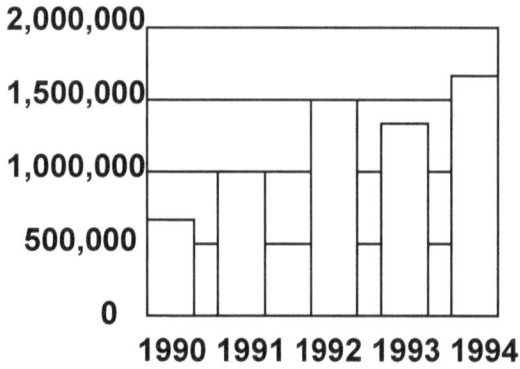

A. 100,000
B. 600,000
C. 1,600,000
D. 8,000,000

Answer: B. 600,000
The number of tourists in 1991 was 1,000,000 and the number in 1994 was 1,600,000. Subtract to get a difference of 600,000.

19. **Consider the graph of the distribution of the length of time it took individuals to complete an employment form.**
(Average)

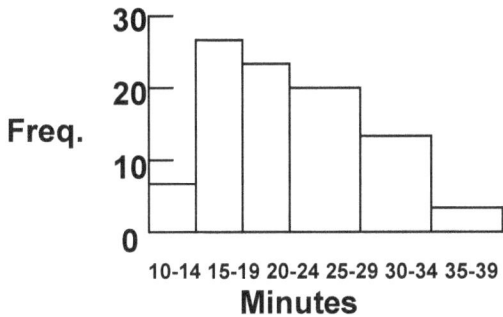

Minutes

Approximately how many individuals took less than 15 minutes to complete the employment form?

A. 35
B. 28
C. 7
D. 4

Answer: C. 7
According to the chart, the number of people who took under 15 minutes is 7.

20. **Which statement is true about George's budget?**
(Easy)

A. George spends the greatest portion of his income on food.
B. George spends twice as much on utilities as he does on his mortgage.
C. George spends twice as much on utilities as he does on food.
D. George spends the same amount on food and utilities as he does on mortgage.

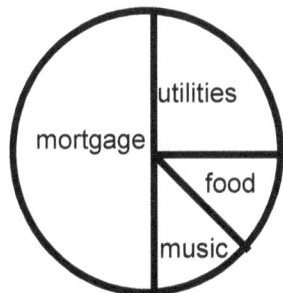

Answer: C. George spends twice as much on utilities as he does on food.
The wedge representing utilities is twice as large as the wedge representing food.

21. **Corporate salaries are listed for several employees. Which is the best measure of central tendency?**
    (Average)

    $24,000 $24,000 $26,000 $28,000 $30,000 $120,000

    A. Mean
    B. Median
    C. Mode
    D. No difference

Answer: B. Median
The median provides the best measure of central tendency in this case where the mode is the lowest number and the mean is disproportionately skewed by the outlier $120,000.

22. **Compute the median for the following data set:**
    (Easy)

    {12, 19, 13, 16, 17, 14}

    A. 14.5
    B. 15.17
    C. 15
    D. 16

Answer: C. 15
Arrange the data in ascending order: 12,13,14,16,17,19. The median is the middle value in a list with an odd number of entries. When there is an even number of entries, the median is the mean of the two center entries. Here the average of 14 and 16 is 15.

23. **State the domain of the function** $f(x) = \dfrac{3x - 6}{x^2 - 25}$

    (Rigorous)

    A. $x \neq 2$
    B. $x \neq 5, -5$
    C. $x \neq 2, -2$
    D. $x \neq 5$

Answer: B. $x \neq 5, -5$
The values of 5 and –5 must be omitted from the domain of all real numbers because if x took on either of those values, the denominator of the fraction would have a value of 0, and therefore the fraction would be undefined.

24. **Which graph represents the equation of** $y = x^2 + 3x$?
(Rigorous)

A.

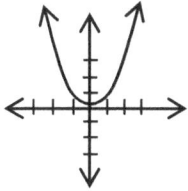

B.

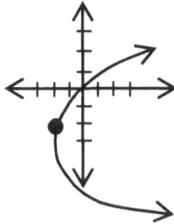

C.

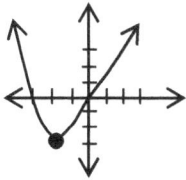

D.

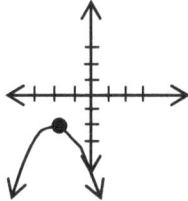

Answer: C.
B is not the graph of a function. D is the graph of a parabola where the coefficient of x^2 is negative. A appears to be the graph of $y = x^2$. To find the x-intercepts of $y = x^2 + 3x$, set $y = 0$ and solve for x: $0 = x^2 + 3x = x(x + 3)$ to get $x = 0$ or $x = -3$. Therefore, the graph of the function intersects the x-axis at x=0 and x=-3.

25. Choose the equation that is equivalent to the following:
(Rigorous)

$$\frac{3x}{5} - 5 = 5x$$

A. $3x - 25 = 25x$

B. $x - \dfrac{25}{3} = 25x$

C. $6x - 50 = 75x$

D. $x + 25 = 25x$

Answer: A. $3x - 25 = 25x$
A is the correct answer because it is the original equation multiplied by 5. The other choices alter the answer to the original equation.

26. If $4x - (3 - x) = 7(x - 3) + 10$, then
(Rigorous)

A. $x = 8$
B. $x = -8$
C. $x = 4$
D. $x = -4$

Answer: C. $x = 4$
Solve for x.

$$4x - (3 - x) = 7(x - 3) + 10$$
$$4x - 3 + x = 7x - 21 + 10$$
$$5x - 3 = 7x - 11$$
$$5x = 7x - 11 + 3$$
$$5x - 7x = {}^-8$$
$${}^-2x = {}^-8$$
$$x = 4$$

27. Solve for x.

$$3x - \frac{2}{3} = \frac{5x}{2} + 2$$

(Rigorous)

A. $5\frac{1}{3}$

B. $\frac{17}{3}$

C. 2

D. $\frac{16}{2}$

Answer: A. $5\frac{1}{3}$

$$3x(6) - \frac{2}{3}(6) = \frac{5x}{2}(6) + 2(6) \qquad \text{6 is the LCD of 2 and 3}$$

$$18x - 4 = 15x + 12$$

$$18x = 15x + 16$$

$$3x = 16$$

$$x = \frac{16}{3} = 5\frac{1}{3}$$

28. Given the formula *d =rt*, (where *d* = distance, *r* =rate, and *t* =time), calculate the time required for a vehicle to travel 585 miles at a rate of 65 miles per hour.
(Average)

A. 8.5 hours
B. 6.5 hours
C. 9.5 hours
D. 9 hours

Answer: D. 9 hours
We are given *d* = 585 miles and *r* = 65 miles per hour and *d* =rt. Solve for *t*.
$585 = 65t \rightarrow t = 9$ hours.

29. **Solve the system of equations** for x, y and z.
   (Rigorous)

   $$3x + 2y - z = 0$$
   $$2x + 5y = 8z$$
   $$x + 3y + 2z = 7$$

   A. $(-1, \ 2, \ 1)$
   B. $(1, \ 2, \ -1)$
   C. $(-3, \ 4, \ -1)$
   D. $(0, \ 1, \ 2)$

Answer: A. $(-1, \ 2, \ 1)$
Multiplying equation 1 by 2, and equation 2 by –3, and then adding together the two resulting equations gives -11y + 22z = 0. Solving for y gives y = 2z. In the meantime, multiplying equation 3 by –2 and adding it to equation 2 gives –y – 12z = -14. Then substituting 2z for y, yields the result z = 1. Subsequently, one can easily find that y = 2, and x = -1.

30. **What is the equation that expresses the relationship between x and y in the table below?**
   (Average)

x	y
-2	4
-1	1
0	-2
1	-5
2	-8

   A. $y = -x - 2$
   B. $y = -3x - 2$
   C. $y = 3x - 2$
   D. $y = \dfrac{1}{3}x - 1$

Answer: B. y = -3x - 2
Solve by plugging the values of x and y into the equations to see if they work. The answer is B because it is the only equation for which the values of x and y are correct.

31. **Choose the expression that is not equivalent to 5x + 3y + 15z:**
(Average)

    A. 5(x + 3z) + 3y
    B. 3(x + y + 5z)
    C. 3y + 5(x + 3z)
    D. 5x + 3(y + 5z)

Answer: B. 3(x + y +5z)

5x + 3y + 15z = (5x + 15z) + 3y = 5(x + 3z) + 3y	A. is true
= 5x + (3y + 15z) = 5x + 3(y + 5z)	D. is true
= 3y + (5x + 15z) = 3y + 5(x + 3z)	C. is true

We can solve all of these using the associative property and then factoring. However, in B 3(x + y + 5z) by distributive property = 3x + 3y + 15z, which does not equal 5x + 3y + 15z.

32. **Simplify:** $\sqrt{27} + \sqrt{75}$
(Average)

    A. $8\sqrt{3}$
    B. 34
    C. $34\sqrt{3}$
    D. $15\sqrt{3}$

Answer: A. $8\sqrt{3}$
Simplifying radicals gives $\sqrt{27} + \sqrt{75} = 3\sqrt{3} + 5\sqrt{3} = 8\sqrt{3}$.

33. **What is the equation of the graph below?**
(Rigorous)

A. $2x + y = 2$
B. $2x - y = -2$
C. $2x - y = 2$
D. $2x + y = -2$

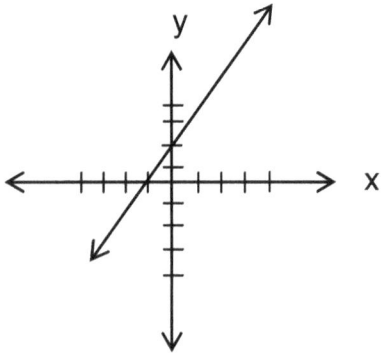

Answer: B. $2x - y = -2$
By observation, we see that the graph has a y-intercept of 2 and a slope of 2/1 = 2. Therefore its equation is y = mx + b = 2x + 2. Rearranging the terms gives 2x − y = -2.

34. $f(x) = 3x - 2; \ f^{-1}(x) =$
(Rigorous)

A. $3x + 2$
B. $x / 6$
C. $2x - 3$
D. $(x + 2) / 3$

Answer: D. $(x + 2) / 3$
To find the inverse, f⁻¹(x), of the given function, reverse the variables in the given equation, y = 3x − 2, to get x = 3y − 2. Then solve for y as follows:
x+2 = 3y, and y = $\dfrac{x + 2}{3}$.

35. **What is the area of a square whose side is 13 feet?**
(Easy)

    A. 169 feet
    B. 169 square feet
    C. 52 feet
    D. 52 square feet

Answer: B. 169 square feet
Area = length times width (*lw*).
Length = 13 feet
Width = 13 feet (square, so length and width are the same).
Area = $13 \times 13 = 169$ square feet.
Area is measured in square feet.

36. **The trunk of a tree has a 2.1 meter radius. What is its circumference?**
(Easy)

    A. 2.1π square meters
    B. 4.2π meters
    C. $2.1\ \pi$ meters
    D. 4.2π square meters

Answer: B. 4.2π meters
Circumference is $2\pi r$, where r is the radius. The circumference is $2\pi 2.1 = 4.2\pi$ meters (not square meters because we are not measuring area).

37. **The figure below shows a running track and the shape of an inscribed rectangle with semicircles at each end.**
   (Rigorous)

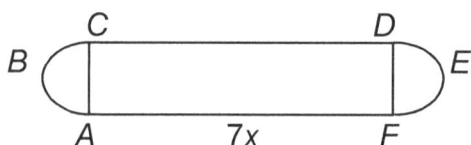

Calculate the distance around the track (r = 1.5y).

A. $6\pi y + 14x$
B. $3\pi y + 7x$
C. $6\pi y + 7x$
D. $3\pi y + 14x$

Answer: D. $3\pi y + 14x$

The two semicircles of the track create one circle with a diameter 3y. The circumference of a circle is $C = \pi d$ so $C = 3\pi y$. The length of both sides of the track is 7x each side, so the total circumference around the track is $3\pi y + 7x + 7x = 3\pi y + 14x$

38. **What type of triangle is triangle ABC?**
   (Easy)

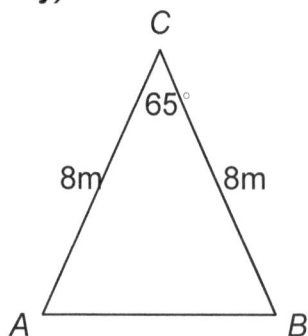

A. right
B. equilateral
C. scalene
D. isosceles

Answer: D. isosceles

Two of the sides are the same length, so we know the triangle is either equilateral or isosceles. $\angle CAB$ and $\angle CBA$ are equal, because their sides are. Therefore, $180° = 65° - 2x = \dfrac{115°}{2} = 57.5°$. Because all three angles are not equal, the triangle is isosceles.

39.   What is the area of this triangle?
(Easy)

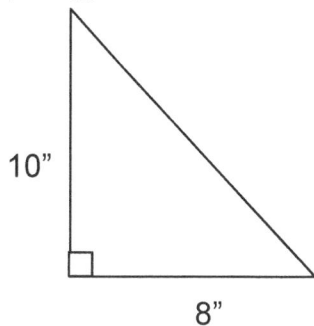

10"

8"

A. 80 square inches
B. 20 square inches
C. 40 square inches
D. 30 square inches

Answer: C. 40 square inches

The area of a triangle is $\frac{1}{2}bh$.

$\frac{1}{2}x8x10 = 40$ square inches.

40.   For the following statements
(Average)

I. All parallelograms are rectangles
II. Some rhombi are squares

A. Both statements are correct
B. Both statements are incorrect
C. Only II is correct
D. Only I is correct

Answer: C. Only II is correct

I is false because only some parallelograms are rectangles. II is true. So only II is correct.

41. **Find the surface area of a box which is 3 feet wide, 5 feet tall, and 4 feet deep.**
(Average)

    A. 47 sq. ft.
    B. 60 sq. ft.
    C. 94 sq. ft
    D. 188 sq. ft.

Answer: C. 94 sq. ft.
Let's assume the base of the rectangular solid (box) is 3 by 4, and the height is 5. Then the surface area of the top and bottom together is 2(12) = 24. The sum of the areas of the front and back are 2(15) = 30, while the sum of the areas of the sides are 2(20) =40. The total surface area is therefore 94 square feet.

42. **The owner of a rectangular piece of land 40 yards in length and 30 yards in width wants to divide it into two parts. She plans to join two opposite corners with a fence as shown in the diagram below. The cost of the fence will be approximately $25 per linear foot. What is the estimated cost for the fence needed by the owner?**
(Rigorous)

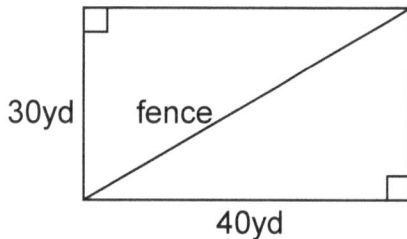

    A. $1,250
    B. $62,500
    C. $5,250
    D. $3,750

Answer: D. $3,750
Find the length of the diagonal by using the Pythagorean theorem. Let x be the length of the diagonal.

$$30^2 + 40^2 = x^2 \rightarrow 900 + 1600 = x^2$$
$$2500 = x^2 \rightarrow \sqrt{2500} = \sqrt{x^2}$$
$$x = 50 \text{ yards}$$

Convert to feet. $\dfrac{50 \text{ yards}}{x \text{ feet}} = \dfrac{1 \text{ yard}}{3 \text{ feet}} \rightarrow 150$ feet

It cost $25.00 per linear foot, so the cost is (150 ft) ($25) = $3750.

43.   Which term most accurately describes two coplanar lines without any common points?
       (Average)

   A. perpendicular
   B. parallel
   C. intersecting
   D. skew

Answer: B. parallel
By definition, parallel lines are coplanar lines without any common points.

44.   **Set A, B, C, and U are related as shown in the diagram.**
       (Rigorous)

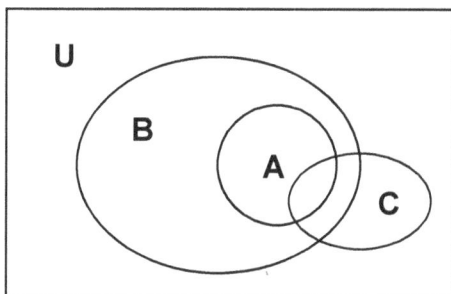

       Which of the following is true, assuming not one of the six regions is empty?

   A. Any element that is a member of set B is also a member of set A.
   B. No element is a member of all three sets A, B, and C.
   C. Any element that is a member of set U is also a member of set B.
   D. None of the above statements is true.

Answer: D. None of the above statements is true.
Answer A is incorrect because not all members of set B are also in set A. Answer B is incorrect because there are elements that are members of all three sets A, B, and C. Answer C is incorrect because not all members of set U are members of set B. This leaves answer D, which states that none of the above choices are true.

45. **Select the statement that is the negation of the statement, "If the weather is cold, then the soccer game will be played."**
(Rigorous)

    A. If the weather is not cold, then the soccer game will be played.
    B. The weather is cold and the soccer game was not played.
    C. If the soccer game is played, then the weather is not cold.
    D. The weather is cold and the soccer game will be played.

Answer: B. The weather is cold and the soccer game was not played.
Negation of "if p, then q" is "p and (not q)". So the negation of the given statement is "The weather is cold and the soccer game was not played ".

46. **Select the statement below that is logically equivalent to "If Mary works late, then Bill will prepare lunch."**
(Rigorous)

    A. Bill prepares lunch or Mary does not work late.
    B. If Bill does not prepare lunch, then Mary did not work late.
    C. If Bill prepares lunch, then Mary works late.
    D. Mary does not work late or Bill prepares lunch.

Answer: B. If Bill does not prepare lunch, then Mary did not work late.
The contrapositive of a statement is always logically equivalent to the statement. The contrapositive of "if p then q" is "if not q then not p". Since statement B is the contrapositive of the given statement, it is logically equivalent.

The other answer choices assume that if Mary does not work late then Bill does not prepare lunch. This is not a valid deduction from the original statement which merely states that Bill prepares lunch when Mary works late. It does not eliminate the possibility that Bill prepares lunch when Mary does not work late. Hence these statements are not logically equivalent to the given statement.

47. **Select the rule of logical equivalence that directly (in one step) transforms the statement (i) into statement (ii),**
(Average)

i. Not all the students have books.
ii. Some students do not have books.

A. "If p, then q" is equivalent to "if not q, then b."
B. "Not all are p" is equivalent to "some are not p."
C. "Not q" is equivalent to "p."
D. "All are not p" is equivalent to "none are p"

Answer: B. "Not all are p" is equivalent to "some are not p."
If we assume that the statement p is "students have books", then "not p" is "students do not have books". It is clear that statements (i) and (ii) are equivalent to the choice B.

48. **Given that:**

i. No athletes are weak.
ii. All football players are athletes.

Determine which conclusion can be logically deduced.
(Average)

A. Some football players are weak.
B. All football players are weak.
C. No football player is weak.
D. None of the above is true.

Answer: C. No football player is weak.
According to the law of syllogism, "if p then q and if q then r" implies "if p then r". We can rephrase the statements above to read:

i. If a person is a football player, he or she is an athlete.
ii. If a person is an athlete, he or she is not weak.

Then, using the law of syllogism, we can conclude:
If a person is a football player, he or she is not weak.
This statement is equivalent to the one in choice C.

49. **Study the information given below. If a logical conclusion is given, select that conclusion.**
(Rigorous)

Bob eats donuts or he eats yogurt. If Bob eats yogurt, then he is healthy. If Bob is healthy, then he can run the marathon. Bob does not eat yogurt.

  A. Bob does not eat donuts.
  B. Bob is healthy.
  C. If Bob runs the marathon then he eats yogurt.
  D. None of the above is warranted.

Answer: D. None of the above is warranted.
Statement A is not warranted since "Bob eats donuts or he eats yogurt" and "Bob does not eat yogurt" implies that "Bob eats donuts".

Statement B is not warranted since according to the given statements, Bob does not eat yogurt and Bob is healthy if he eats yogurt. The statements do not say anything about Bob's health if he does not eat yogurt.

Statement C is not warranted since Bob may run the marathon even if he does not eat yogurt. The given statements do not say anything about Bob's ability to run the marathon if he does not eat yogurt. It merely implies that he can run the marathon if he does eat yogurt.

50. **Given $K(-4, y)$ and $M(2, -3)$ with midpoint $L(x, 1)$, determine the values of x and y.**
(Rigorous)

  A. $x = -1, \ y = 5$
  B. $x = 3, \ y = 2$
  C. $x = 5, \ y = -1$
  D. $x = -1, \ y = -1$

Answer: A. $x = -1, \ y = 5$
The formula for finding the midpoint (a,b) of a segment passing through the points $(x_1, y_1) \, and \, (x_2, y_2) \, is \, (a, b) = (\frac{x_1 + x_2}{2}, \frac{y_1 + y_2}{2})$. Setting up the corresponding equations from this information gives us $x = \frac{-4 + 2}{2}, \, and \, 1 = \frac{y - 3}{2}$. Solving for x and y gives x = -1 and y = 5.

ELEMENTS OF COMPOSITION

Directions: The passage below contains many errors. Read the passage. Then, answer each test item by choosing the option that corrects an error in the underlined portion(s). No more than one underlined error will appear in each item. If no error exists, choose "No change is necessary."

Climbing to the top of Mount Everest is an adventure. One which everyone--whether physically fit or not--seems eager to try. The trail stretches for miles, the cold temperatures are usually frigid and brutal.

Climbers must endure severel barriers on the way, including other hikers, steep jagged rocks, and lots of snow. Plus, climbers often find the most grueling part of the trip is their climb back down, just when they are feeling greatly exhausted. Climbers who take precautions are likely to find the ascent less arduous than the unprepared. By donning heavy flannel shirts, gloves, and hats, climbers prevented hypothermia, as well as simple frostbite. A pair of rugged boots is also one of the necesities. If climbers are to avoid becoming dehydrated, there is beverages available for them to transport as well.

Once climbers are completely ready to begin their lengthy journey, they can comfortable enjoy the wonderful scenery. Wide rock formations dazzle the observers eyes with shades of gray and white, while the peak forms a triangle that seems to touch the sky. Each of the climbers are reminded of the splendor and magnificence of God's great Earth.

1. **If climbers are to avoid <u>becoming</u> dehydrated, there <u>is</u> beverages available for <u>them</u> to transport as well.**
   (Rigorous)

   A. becomming
   B. are
   C. him
   D. No change is necessary.

2. **Each of the climbers <u>are</u> reminded of the splendor and <u>magnificence</u> of <u>God's</u> great Earth.**
   (Rigorous)

   A. is
   B. magnifisence
   C. Gods
   D. No change is necessary.

3. **Climbing to the top of Mount Everest is an <u>adventure. One</u> which everyone <u>—whether</u> physically fit or not—<u>seems</u> eager to try.**
   (Average)

   A. adventure, one
   B. everyone, whether
   C. seem
   D. No change is necessary.

4. **A pair of rugged boots <u>is also one</u> of the <u>necesities</u>.**
    (Average)

    A. are
    B. also, one
    C. necessities
    D. No change is necessary.

5. **Plus, climbers often find the most grueling part of the trip is <u>their</u> climb back <u>down, just</u> when they <u>are</u> feeling greatly exhausted.**
    (Rigorous)

    A. his
    B. down; just
    C. were
    D. No change is necessary.

6. **By donning heavy flannel shirts, boots, and <u>hats, climbers</u> <u>prevented</u> hypothermia, as well as simple frostbite.**
    (Average)

    A. hats climbers
    B. can prevent
    C. hypothermia;
    D. No change is necessary.

7. **Climbers must endure <u>severel</u> barriers <u>on the way, including</u> other <u>hikers,</u> steep jagged rocks, and lots of snow.**
    (Average)

    A. several
    B. on the way: including
    C. hikers'
    D. No change is necessary.

8. **<u>Climbers who</u> take precautions are likely to find the ascent <u>less difficult than</u> the unprepared.**
    (Easy)

    A. Climbers, who
    B. least difficult
    C. then
    D. No change is necessary.

9. **Once climbers are completely prepared for <u>their</u> lengthy <u>journey, they</u> can <u>comfortable</u> enjoy the wonderful scenery.**
    (Easy)

    A. they're
    B. journey; they
    C. comfortably
    D. No change is necessary.

10. **Wide rock formations dazzle the <u>observers eyes</u> with shades of gray and <u>white, while</u> the peak forms a triangle that seems to touch the sky.**
    (Average)

    A. observers' eyes
    B. white; while
    C. formed
    D. No change is necessary.

11. **The <u>trail</u> stretches for <u>miles,</u> the cold temperatures are <u>usually</u> frigid and brutal.**
    (Rigorous)

    A. trails
    B. miles;
    C. usual
    D. No change is necessary.

Directions: The passage below contains several errors. Read the passage. Then, answer each test item by choosing the option that corrects an error in the underlined portion(s). No more than one underlined error will appear in each item. If no error exists, choose "No change is necessary."

Every job places different kinds of demands on their employees. For example, whereas such jobs as accounting and bookkeeping require mathematical ability; graphic design requires creative/artistic ability.

Doing good at one job does not usually guarantee success at another. However, one of the elements crucial to all jobs are especially notable: the chance to accomplish a goal.

The accomplishment of the employees varies according to the job. In many jobs, the employees become accustom to the accomplishment provided by the work they do every day.

In medicine, for example, every doctor tests him self by treating badly injured or critically ill people. In the operating room, a team of Surgeons, is responsible for operating on many of these patients. In addition to the feeling of accomplishment that the workers achieve, some jobs also give a sense of identity to the employees'. Profesions like law, education, and sales offer huge financial and emotional rewards. Politicians are public servants: who work for the federal and state governments.

President obama is basically employed by the American people to make laws and run the country.

Finally; the contributions that employees make to their companies and to the world cannot be taken for granted. Through their work, employees are performing a service for their employers and are contributing something to the world.

12. **Every job <u>places</u> different kinds of demands on <u>their</u> <u>employees</u>.**
   (Average)

   A. place
   B. its
   C. employes
   D. No change is necessary.

13. **<u>However,</u> one of the elements crucial to all jobs <u>are</u> especially <u>notable:</u> the accomplishment of a goal.**
   (Average)

   A. However
   B. is
   C. notable;
   D. No change is necessary.

14. **The <u>accomplishment</u> of the <u>employees</u> <u>varies</u> according to the job.**
   (Average)

   A. accomplishment,
   B. employee's
   C. vary
   D. No change is necessary.

15. <u>Profesions</u> like law, <u>education,</u> and sales <u>offer</u> huge financial and emotional rewards.
(Easy)

A. Professions
B. education;
C. offered
D. No change is necessary.

16. Doing <u>good</u> at one job does not <u>usually</u> guarantee <u>success</u> at another.
(Average)

A. well
B. usualy
C. succeeding
D. No change is necessary.

17. In many jobs, the employees <u>become accustom</u> to the accomplishment <u>provided</u> by the work they do every day.
(Rigorous)

A. became
B. accustomed
C. provides
D. No change is necessary.

18. In medicine, for example, every doctor <u>tests</u> <u>him self</u> by treating badly-injured and critically ill people.
(Easy)

A. test
B. himself
C. critical
D. No change is necessary.

19. In addition to the feeling of accomplishment that the workers <u>achieve,</u> some jobs also <u>give</u> a sense of self-identity to the <u>employees'.</u>
(Average)

A. acheve
B. gave
C. employees
D. No change is necessary.

20. <u>For example, whereas</u> such jobs as accounting and bookkeeping require mathematical <u>ability;</u> graphic design requires creative/artistic ability.
(Rigorous)

A. For example
B. whereas,
C. ability,
D. No change is necessary.

21. In the <u>operating room, a</u> team of <u>Surgeons, is</u> responsible for operating on many of <u>these</u> patients.
(Easy)

A. operating room:
B. surgeons is
C. those
D. No change is necessary.

22. Politicians <u>are</u> public <u>servants: who work</u> for the federal and state governments.
(Average)

A. were
B. servants who
C. worked
D. No change is necessary.

23. **President obama is basically employed <u>by</u> the American people to <u>make</u> laws and run the country.**
(Easy)

A. Obama
B. to
C. made
D. No change is necessary.

24. **<u>Finally;</u> the contributions that employees make to <u>their</u> companies and to the world cannot be <u>taken</u> for granted.**
(Average)

A. Finally,
B. thier
C. took
D. No change is necessary.

Directions: For the underlined sentence(s), choose the option that expresses the meaning with the most fluency and the clearest logic within the context. If the underlined sentence should not be changed, choose Option A, which shows no change.

25. **Which of the following sentences logically and correctly expresses the comparison?**
(Rigorous)

A. The Empire State Building in New York is taller than buildings in the city.
B. The Empire State Building in New York is taller than any other building in the city.
C. The Empire State Building in New York is tallest than other buildings in the city.

26. **Treating patients for drug and/or alcohol abuse is a sometimes difficult process.** <u>**Even though there are a number of different methods for helping the patient overcome a dependency, there is no way of knowing which is best in the long run.**</u>
(Rigorous)

   A. Even though there are a number of different methods for helping the patient overcome a dependency, there is no way of knowing which is best in the long run.

   B. Even though different methods can help a patient overcome a dependency, there is no way to know which is best in the long run.

   C. Even though there is no way to know which way is best in the long run, patients can overcome their dependencies when they are helped.

   D. There is no way to know which method will help the patient overcome a dependency in the long run, even though there are many different ones.

27. **Selecting members of a President's cabinet can often be an aggravating process.** <u>**Either there are too many or too few qualified candidates for a certain position, and then they have to be confirmed by the Senate, where there is the possibility of rejection.**</u>
(Rigorous)

   A. Either there are too many or too few qualified candidates for a certain position, and then they have to be confirmed by the Senate, where there is the possibility of rejection.

   B. Qualified candidates for certain positions face the possibility of rejection, when they have to be confirmed by the Senate.

   C. The Senate has to confirm qualified candidates, who face the possibility of rejection.

   D. Because the Senate has to confirm qualified candidates; they face the possibility of rejection.

28. **Many factors account for the decline in the quality of public education.** <u>**Overcrowding, budget cutbacks, and societal deterioration which have greatly affected student learning**</u>.
(Rigorous)

   A. Overcrowding, budget cutbacks, and societal deterioration which have greatly affected student learning.
   B. Student learning has been greatly affected by overcrowding, budget cutbacks, and societal deterioration.
   C. Due to overcrowding, budget cutbacks, and societal deterioration, student learning has been greatly affected.
   D. Overcrowding, budget cutbacks, and societal deterioration have affected students learning greatly.

Directions: Choose the most effective word within the context of the sentence.

29. **Many of the clubs in Boca Raton are noted for their _____ elegance.**
(Average)

   A. vulgar
   B. tasteful
   C. ordinary

30. **When a student is expelled from school, the parents are usually _____ in advance.**
(Easy)

   A. rewarded
   B. congratulated
   C. notified

31. **Before appearing in court, the witness was _____ the papers requiring her to show up.**
(Easy)

   A. condemned
   B. served
   C. criticized

Directions: Choose the underlined word or phrase that is unnecessary within the context of the passage.

32. <u>Considered by many to be</u> one of the worst <u>terrorist</u> incidents <u>on American soil</u> was the bombing of the Oklahoma City Federal Building, which will be remembered <u>for years to come</u>.
(Rigorous)

    A. considered by many to be
    B. terrorist
    C. on American soil
    D. for years to come

33. The <u>flu</u> epidemic struck <u>most of</u> the <u>respected</u> faculty and students of The Woolbright School, forcing the Boynton Beach School Superintendent to close it down <u>for two weeks</u>.
(Rigorous)

    A. flu
    B. most of
    C. respected
    D. for two weeks

34. The <u>expanding</u> number of television channels has <u>prompted</u> cable operators to raise their prices, <u>even though</u> many consumers do not want to pay a higher <u>increased</u> amount for their service.
(Average)

    A. expanding
    B. prompted
    C. even though
    D. increased

Directions: The passage below contains several errors. Read the passage. Then, answer each test item by choosing the option that corrects an error in the underlined portion(s). No more than one underlined error will appear in each item. If no error exists, choose "No change is necessary."

The discovery of a body at Paris Point marina in Boca Raton shocked the residents of Palmetto Pines, a luxury condominium complex located next door to the marina.

The victim is a thirty-five year old woman who had been apparently bludgeoned to death and dumped in the ocean late last night. Many neighbors reported terrible screams, gunshots: as well as the sound of a car backfiring loudly to Boca Raton Police shortly after midnight. The woman had been spotted in the lobby of Palmetto Pines around ten thirty, along with an older man, estimated to be in his fifties, and a younger man, in his late twenties.

"Apparently, the victim had been driven to the complex by the older man and was seen arguing with him when the younger man intervened," said Sheriff Fred Adams, "all three of them left the building together and walked to the marina, where gunshots rang out an hour later." Deputies found five bullets on the sidewalk and some blood, along with a steel pipe that is assumed to be the murder weapon. Two men were seen fleeing the scene in a red Mercedes shortly after, rushing toward the Interstate. The Palm Beach County Coroner, Melvin

Watts, said he concluded the victim's skull had been crushed by a blunt tool, which resulted in a brain hemorrhage. As of now, there is no clear motive for the murder.

35. The victim <u>is</u> a thirty-five-year-old who had been apparently <u>bludgeoned</u> to death and dumped in the <u>ocean late</u> last night.
(Rigorous)

   A. was
   B. bludgoned
   C. ocean: late
   D. No change is necessary.

36. The discovery of a body at Paris Point <u>marina</u> in Boca Raton shocked the <u>residents</u> of Palmetto Pines, a luxury <u>condominium</u> complex located next door to the marina.
(Rigorous)

   A. Marina
   B. residence
   C. condominnium
   D. No change is necessary.

37. Deputies found five bullets on the sidewalk and some <u>blood,</u> along with a steel pipe that is <u>assumed</u> <u>to be</u> the murder weapon.
(Rigorous)

   A. blood;
   B. assuming
   C. to have been
   D. No change is necessary.

38. Many <u>neighbors</u> reported terrible screams, <u>gunshots:</u> <u>as</u> well as the sound of a car, backfiring <u>loudly</u> to Boca Raton Police shortly after midnight.
(Average)

A. nieghbors
B. gunshots, as
C. loud
D. No change is necessary.

39. The woman <u>had</u> been spotted in the lobby of Palmetto Pines around ten <u>thirty,</u> along with an older <u>man, estimated</u> to be in his fifties, and a younger man in his late twenties.
(Average)

A. has
B. thirty;
C. man estimated
D. No change is necessary.

40. "Apparently, the victim had been driven to the complex by the older man and was seen arguing with him when the younger man intervened," said <u>Sheriff Fred Adams, "all</u> three of them left the building together and walked to the marina, where gunshots rang out an hour later."
(Rigorous)

A. sheriff Fred Adams, "all
B. sheriff Fred Adams, "All
C. Sheriff Fred Adams. "All
D. No change is necessary.

Answer Key

1.	B	21.	B
2.	A	22.	B
3.	A	23.	A
4.	C	24.	A
5.	D	25.	B
6.	B	26.	B
7.	A	27.	C
8.	D	28.	B
9.	C	29.	B
10.	A	30.	C
11.	B	31.	B
12.	B	32.	A
13.	B	33.	C
14.	C	34.	D
15.	A	35.	A
16.	A	36.	A
17.	B	37.	C
18.	B	38.	B
19.	C	39.	C
20.	C	40.	C

Rigor Table

Easy
8, 9, 15, 18, 21, 23, 30, 31

Average
3, 4, 6, 7, 10, 12, 13, 14, 16, 19, 22, 24, 29, 34, 38, 39

Rigorous
1, 2, 5, 11, 17, 20, 25, 26, 27, 28, 32, 33, 35, 36, 37, 40

ELEMENTS OF COMPOSITION RATIONALES

Directions: The passage below contains many errors. Read the passage. Then, answer each test item by choosing the option that corrects an error in the underlined portion(s). No more than one underlined error will appear in each item. If no error exists, choose "No change is necessary."

Climbing to the top of Mount Everest is an adventure. One which everyone--whether physically fit or not--seems eager to try. The trail stretches for miles, the cold temperatures are usually frigid and brutal.

Climbers must endure severel barriers on the way, including other hikers, steep jagged rocks, and lots of snow. Plus, climbers often find the most grueling part of the trip is their climb back down, just when they are feeling greatly exhausted. Climbers who take precautions are likely to find the ascent less arduous than the unprepared. By donning heavy flannel shirts, gloves, and hats, climbers prevented hypothermia, as well as simple frostbite. A pair of rugged boots is also one of the necesities. If climbers are to avoid becoming dehydrated, there is beverages available for them to transport as well.

Once climbers are completely ready to begin their lengthy journey, they can comfortable enjoy the wonderful scenery. Wide rock formations dazzle the observers eyes with shades of gray and white, while the peak forms a triangle that seems to touch the sky. Each of the climbers are reminded of the splendor and magnificence of God's great Earth.

1. **If climbers are to avoid <u>becoming</u> dehydrated, there <u>is</u> beverages available for <u>them</u> to transport as well.**
    (Rigorous)

    A. becommming
    B. are
    C. him
    D. No change is necessary.

Answer: B. are
The plural verb *are* must be used with the plural subject *beverages*. Option A is incorrect because *becoming* has only one *m*. Option C is incorrect because the plural pronoun *them* is needed to agree with the referent *climbers*.

2.	Each of the climbers <u>are</u> reminded of the splendor and <u>magnificence</u> of <u>God's</u> great Earth.
	(Rigorous)

	A. is
	B. magnifisence
	C. Gods
	D. No change is necessary.

Answer: A. is
The singular verb *is* agrees with the singular subject *each.* Option B is incorrect because *magnificence* is misspelled. Option C is incorrect because an apostrophe is needed to show possession.

3.	Climbing to the top of Mount Everest is an <u>adventure. One</u> which everyone —<u>whether</u> physically fit or not—<u>seems</u> eager to try.
	(Average)

	A. adventure, one
	B. everyone, whether
	C. seem
	D. No change is necessary.

Answer: A. adventure, one
A comma is needed between *adventure* and *one* to avoid creating a fragment of the second part. In Option B, a comma after *everyone* would not be appropriate when the dash is used on the other side of *not*. In Option C, the singular verb *seems* is needed to agree with the singular subject *everyone*.

4.	A pair of rugged boots <u>is</u> also <u>one</u> of the <u>necesities</u>.
	(Average)

	A. are
	B. also, one
	C. necessities
	D. No change is necessary.

Answer: C. necessities
The word *necessities* is misspelled in the text. Option A is incorrect because the singular verb *is* must agree with the singular noun *pair* (a collective singular). Option B is incorrect because *is also* is set off with commas (potential correction); it should be set off on both sides.

5.   Plus, climbers often find the most grueling part of the trip is their climb back down, just when they are feeling greatly exhausted. *(Rigorous)*

   A. his
   B. down; just
   C. were
   D. No change is necessary.

Answer: D. No change is necessary.
The present tense must be used consistently throughout; therefore, Option C is incorrect. Option A is incorrect because the singular pronoun *his* does not agree with the plural antecedent *climbers*. Option B is incorrect because a comma, not a semicolon, is needed to separate the dependent clause from the main clause.

6.   By donning heavy flannel shirts, boots, and hats, climbers prevented hypothermia, as well as simple frostbite. *(Average)*

   A. hats climbers
   B. can prevent
   C. hypothermia;
   D. No change is necessary.

Answer: B. can prevent
The verb *prevented* is in the past tense and must be changed to the present *can prevent* to be consistent. Option A is incorrect because a comma is needed after a long introductory phrase. Option C is incorrect because the semicolon creates a fragment of the phrase *as well as simple frostbite*.

7.   Climbers must endure severel barriers on the way, including other hikers, steep jagged rocks, and lots of snow. *(Average)*

   A. several
   B. on the way: including
   C. hikers'
   D. No change is necessary.

Answer: A. several
The word *several* is misspelled in the text. Option B is incorrect because a comma, not a colon, is needed to set off the modifying phrase. Option C is incorrect because no apostrophe is needed after *hikers* since possession is not involved.

8.　**Climbers who take precautions are likely to find the ascent less difficult than the unprepared.**
(Easy)

    A. Climbers, who
    B. least difficult
    C. then
    D. No change is necessary.

Answer: D. No change is necessary.
No change is needed. Option A is incorrect because a comma would make the phrase *who take precautions* seem less restrictive or less essential to the sentence. Option B is incorrect because *less* is appropriate when two items—the prepared and the unprepared—are compared. Option C is incorrect because the comparative adverb *than*, not *then*, is needed.

9.　**Once climbers are completely prepared for their lengthy journey, they can comfortable enjoy the wonderful scenery.**
(Easy)

    A. they're
    B. journey; they
    C. comfortably
    D. No change is necessary.

Answer: C. comfortably
The adverb form *comfortably* is needed to modify the verb phrase *can enjoy*. Option A is incorrect because the possessive plural pronoun is spelled *their*. Option B is incorrect because a semicolon would make the first half of the item seem like an independent clause when the subordinating conjunction *once* makes that clause dependent.

10. **Wide rock formations dazzle the <u>observers eyes</u> with shades of gray and <u>white, while</u> the peak <u>forms</u> a triangle that seems to touch the sky.**
(Average)

    A. observers' eyes
    B. white; while
    C. formed
    D. No change is necessary.

Answer: A. observers' eyes
An apostrophe is needed to show the plural possessive form *observers' eyes*. Option B is incorrect because the semicolon would make the second half of the item seem like an independent clause when the subordinating conjunction *while* makes that clause dependent. Option C is incorrect because *formed* is in the wrong tense.

11. **The <u>trail</u> stretches for <u>miles</u>, the cold temperatures are <u>usually</u> frigid and brutal.**
(Rigorous)

    A. trails
    B. miles;
    C. usual
    D. No change is necessary.

Answer: B. miles;
A semicolon, not a comma, is needed to separate the first independent clause from the second independent clause. Option A is incorrect because the plural subject *trails* needs the singular verb *stretch*. Option C is incorrect because the adverb form *usually* is needed to modify the adjective *frigid*.

Directions: The passage below contains several errors. Read the passage. Then, answer each test item by choosing the option that corrects an error in the underlined portion(s). No more than one underlined error will appear in each item. If no error exists, choose "No change is necessary."

Every job places different kinds of demands on their employees. For example, whereas such jobs as accounting and bookkeeping require mathematical ability; graphic design requires creative/artistic ability.

Doing good at one job does not usually guarantee success at another. However, one of the elements crucial to all jobs are especially notable: the chance to accomplish a goal.

The accomplishment of the employees varies according to the job. In many jobs, the employees become accustom to the accomplishment provided by the work they do every day.

In medicine, for example, every doctor tests him self by treating badly injured or critically ill people. In the operating room, a team of Surgeons, is responsible for operating on many of these patients. In addition to the feeling of accomplishment that the workers achieve, some jobs also give a sense of identity to the employees'. Profesions like law, education, and sales offer huge financial and emotional rewards. Politicians are public servants: who work for the federal and state governments. President obama is basically employed by the American people to make laws and run the country.

Finally; the contributions that employees make to their companies and to the world cannot be taken for granted. Through their work, employees are performing a service for their employers and are contributing something to the world.

12.   Every job <u>places</u> different kinds of demands on <u>their</u> <u>employees</u>. *(Average)*

    A. place
    B. its
    C. employes
    D. No change is necessary.

Answer: B. its
The singular possessive pronoun *its* must agree with its antecedent *job*, which is singular also. Option A is incorrect because *place* is a plural form, and the subject*, job*, is singular. Option C is incorrect because the correct spelling of employees is given in the sentence.

13. **However,** one of the elements crucial to all jobs **are** especially **notable:** the accomplishment of a goal.
(Average)

    A. However
    B. is
    C. notable;
    D. No change is necessary.

Answer: B. is
The singular verb *is* is needed to agree with the singular subject *one.* Option A is incorrect because a comma is needed to set off the transitional word *however.* Option C is incorrect because a colon, not a semicolon, is needed to set off an item.

14. The **accomplishment** of the **employees** **varies** according to the job.
(Average)

    A. accomplishment,
    B. employee's
    C. vary
    D. No change is necessary.

Answer: C. vary
The singular verb *vary* is needed to agree with the singular subject *accomplishment.* Option A is incorrect because a comma after *accomplishment* would suggest that the modifying phrase *of the employees* is additional instead of essential. Option B is incorrect because *employees* is not possessive.

15. **Profesions** like law, **education,** and sales **offer** huge financial and emotional rewards.
(Easy)

    A. Professions
    B. education;
    C. offered
    D. No change is necessary.

Answer: A. Professions
Option A is correct because *professions* is misspelled in the sentence. Option B is incorrect because a comma, not a semi-colon, is needed after *education.* In Option C, *offered* is in the wrong tense.

16. Doing <u>good</u> at one job does not <u>usually</u> guarantee <u>success</u> at another.
(Average)

    A. well
    B. usualy
    C. succeeding
    D. No change is necessary.

Answer: A. well
The adverb *well* modifies the word *doing*. Option B is incorrect because *usually* is spelled correctly in the sentence. Option C is incorrect because *succeeding* is in the wrong tense.

17. In many jobs, the employees <u>become</u> <u>accustom</u> to the accomplishment <u>provided</u> by the work they do every day.
(Rigorous)

    A. became
    B. accustomed
    C. provides
    D. No change is necessary.

Answer: B. accustomed
The past participle *accustomed* is needed with the verb *become*. Option A is incorrect because the verb tense does not need to change to the past *became*. Option C is incorrect because *provides* is the wrong tense.

18. In medicine, for example, every doctor <u>tests</u> <u>him self</u> by treating badly-injured and critically ill people.
(Easy)

    A. test
    B. himself
    C. critical
    D. No change is necessary.

Answer: B. himself
The reflexive pronoun *himself* is needed. (Him self is nonstandard and never correct.) Option A is incorrect because the singular verb *test* is needed to agree with the singular subject *doctor*. Option C is incorrect because the adverb *critically* is needed to modify the verb *ill*.

19. **In addition to the feeling of accomplishment that the workers achieve, some jobs also give a sense of self-identity to the employees'.**
(Average)

  A. acheve
  B. gave
  C. employees
  D. No change is necessary.

Answer: C. employees
Option C is correct because *employees* is not possessive. Option A is incorrect because *achieve* is spelled correctly in the sentence. Option B is incorrect because *gave* is the wrong tense.

20. **For example, whereas such jobs as accounting and bookkeeping require mathematical ability; graphic design requires creative/artistic ability.**
(Rigorous)

  A. For example
  B. whereas,
  C. ability,
  D. No change is necessary.

Answer: C. ability,
An introductory dependent clause is set off with a comma, not a semicolon. Option A is incorrect because the transitional phrase *for example* should be set off with a comma. Option B is incorrect because the adverb *whereas* functions like *while* and does not take a comma after it.

21. **In the operating room, a team of Surgeons, is responsible for operating on many of these patients.**
(Easy)

  A. operating room:
  B. surgeons is
  C. those
  D. No change is necessary.

Answer: B. surgeons is
Surgeons is not a proper name, so it does not need to be capitalized. A comma is not needed to break up *a team of surgeons* from the rest of the sentence. Option A is incorrect because a comma, not a colon, is needed to set off an item. Option C is incorrect because *those* is an incorrect pronoun.

22. Politicians <u>are</u> public <u>servants: who</u> <u>work</u> for the federal and state governments.
(Average)

    A. were
    B. servants who
    C. worked
    D. No change is necessary.

Answer: B. servants who
A colon is not needed to set off the introduction of the sentence. In Option A, *were* is the incorrect tense of the verb. In Option C, *worked* is in the wrong tense.

23. President obama is basically employed <u>by</u> the American people to <u>make</u> laws and run the country.
(Easy)

    A. Obama
    B. to
    C. made
    D. No change is necessary.

Answer: A. Obama
Obama is a proper name and should be capitalized. In Option B, *to* does not fit with the verb *employed*. Option C uses the wrong form of the verb *make*.

24. <u>Finally;</u> the contributions that employees make to <u>their</u> companies and to the world cannot be <u>taken</u> for granted.
(Average)

    A. Finally,
    B. thier
    C. took
    D. No change is necessary.

Answer: A. Finally,
A comma is needed to separate *Finally* from the rest of the sentence. *Finally* is a preposition which usually heads a dependent sentence, hence a comma is needed. Option B is incorrect because *their* is misspelled. Option C is incorrect because *took* is the wrong form of the verb.

Directions: For the underlined sentence(s), choose the option that expresses the meaning with the most fluency and the clearest logic within the context. If the underlined sentence should not be changed, choose Option A, which shows no change.

25. **Which of the following sentences logically and correctly expresses the comparison?**
    (Rigorous)

    A. The Empire State Building in New York is taller than buildings in the city.
    B. The Empire State Building in New York is taller than any other building in the city.
    C. The Empire State Building in New York is tallest than other buildings in the city.

Answer: B. The Empire State Building in New York is taller than any other building in the city.

Because the Empire State Building is a building in New York City, the phrase *any other* must be included. Option A is incorrect because the Empire State Building is implicitly compared to itself since it is one of the buildings. Option C is incorrect because *tallest* is the incorrect form of the adjective.

26. **Treating patients for drug and/or alcohol abuse is a sometimes difficult process. Even though there are a number of different methods for helping the patient overcome a dependency, there is no way of knowing which is best in the long run.**
(Rigorous)

A. Even though there are a number of different methods for helping the patient overcome a dependency, there is no way of knowing which is best in the long run.
B. Even though different methods can help a patient overcome a dependency, there is no way to know which is best in the long run.
C. Even though there is no way to know which way is best in the long run, patients can overcome their dependencies when they are helped.
D. There is no way to know which method will help the patient overcome a dependency in the long run, even though there are many different ones.

Answer: B. Even though different methods can help a patient overcome a dependency, there is no way to know which is best in the long run.
Option B is concise and logical. Option A tends to ramble with the use of *there are* and the verbs *helping* and *knowing*. Option C is awkwardly worded and repetitive in the first part of the sentence, and vague in the second because it never indicates how the patients can be helped. Option D contains the unnecessary phrase *even though there are many different ones.*

27. **Selecting members of a President's cabinet can often be an aggravating process. <u>Either there are too many or too few qualified candidates for a certain position, and then they have to be confirmed by the Senate, where there is the possibility of rejection.</u>**
(Rigorous)

   A. Either there are too many or too few qualified candidates for a certain position, and then they have to be confirmed by the Senate, where there is the possibility of rejection.
   B. Qualified candidates for certain positions face the possibility of rejection, when they have to be confirmed by the Senate.
   C. The Senate has to confirm qualified candidates, who face the possibility of rejection.
   D. Because the Senate has to confirm qualified candidates; they face the possibility of rejection.

Answer: C. The Senate has to confirm qualified candidates, who face the possibility of rejection.
Option C is the most straightforward and concise sentence. Option A is too unwieldy with the wordy *Either...or* phrase at the beginning. Option B doesn't make clear the fact that candidates face rejection by the Senate. Option D illogically implies that candidates face rejection because they have to be confirmed by the Senate.

28. **Many factors account for the decline in the quality of public education. <u>Overcrowding, budget cutbacks, and societal deterioration which have greatly affected student learning.</u>**
(Rigorous)

   A. Overcrowding, budget cutbacks, and societal deterioration which have greatly affected student learning.
   B. Student learning has been greatly affected by overcrowding, budget cutbacks, and societal deterioration.
   C. Due to overcrowding, budget cutbacks, and societal deterioration, student learning has been greatly affected.
   D. Overcrowding, budget cutbacks, and societal deterioration have affected students learning greatly.

Answer: B. Student learning has been greatly affected by overcrowding, budget cutbacks, and societal deterioration.
Option B is concise and best explains the causes of the decline in student education. The unnecessary use of *which* in Option A makes the sentence feel incomplete. Option C has weak coordination between the reasons for the decline in public education and the fact that student learning has been affected. Option D incorrectly places the adverb *greatly* after learning, instead of before *affected.*

Directions: Choose the most effective word within the context of the sentence.

29. Many of the clubs in Boca Raton are noted for their _____ elegance.
    (Average)

    A. vulgar
    B. tasteful
    C. ordinary

Answer: B. tasteful
Tasteful means beautiful or charming, which would correspond to an elegant club. The words *vulgar* and *ordinary* have negative connotations.

30. When a student is expelled from school, the parents are usually _____ in advance.
    (Easy)

    A. rewarded
    B. congratulated
    C. notified

Answer: C. notified
Notified means informed or told, which fits into the logic of the sentence. The words *rewarded* and *congratulated* are positive actions, which don't make sense regarding someone being expelled from school.

31. Before appearing in court, the witness was _____ the papers requiring her to show up.
    (Easy)

    A. condemned
    B. served
    C. criticized

Answer: B. served
Served means given, which makes sense in the context of the sentence. *Condemned* and *criticized* do not make sense within the context of the sentence.

Directions: Choose the underlined word or phrase that is unnecessary within the context of the passage.

32.   <u>Considered by many to be</u> one of the worst <u>terrorist</u> incidents <u>on American soil</u> was the bombing of the Oklahoma City Federal Building, which will be remembered <u>for years to come</u>.
       (Rigorous)

       A. considered by many to be
       B. terrorist
       C. on American soil
       D. for years to come

Answer: A. considered by many to be
Considered by many to be is a wordy phrase and unnecessary in the context of the sentence. All other words are necessary within the context of the sentence.

33.   The <u>flu</u> epidemic struck <u>most of</u> the <u>respected</u> faculty and students of The Woolbright School, forcing the Boynton Beach School Superintendent to close it down <u>for two weeks.</u>
       (Rigorous)

       A. flu
       B. most of
       C. respected
       D. for two weeks

Answer: C. respected
The fact that the faculty might have been *respected* is not really necessary to mention in the sentence. The other words and phrases are all necessary to complete the meaning of the sentence. The correct answer is C.

34.   The <u>expanding</u> number of television channels has <u>prompted</u> cable operators to raise their prices, <u>even though</u> many consumers do not want to pay a higher <u>increased</u> amount for their service.
       (Average)

       A. expanding
       B. prompted
       C. even though
       D. increased

Answer: D. increased
The word *increased* is redundant with *higher* and should be removed. All the other words are necessary within the context of the sentence.

Directions: The passage below contains several errors. Read the passage. Then, answer each test item by choosing the option that corrects an error in the underlined portion(s). No more than one underlined error will appear in each item. If no error exists, choose "No change is necessary."

The discovery of a body at Paris Point marina in Boca Raton shocked the residents of Palmetto Pines, a luxury condominium complex located next door to the marina.

The victim is a thirty-five year old woman who had been apparently bludgeoned to death and dumped in the ocean late last night. Many neighbors reported terrible screams, gunshots: as well as the sound of a car backfiring loudly to Boca Raton Police shortly after midnight. The woman had been spotted in the lobby of Palmetto Pines around ten thirty, along with an older man, estimated to be in his fifties, and a younger man, in his late twenties.

"Apparently, the victim had been driven to the complex by the older man and was seen arguing with him when the younger man intervened," said Sheriff Fred Adams, "all three of them left the building together and walked to the marina, where gunshots rang out an hour later." Deputies found five bullets on the sidewalk and some blood, along with a steel pipe that is assumed to be the murder weapon. Two men were seen fleeing the scene in a red Mercedes shortly after, rushing toward the Interstate. The Palm Beach County Coroner, Melvin Watts, said he concluded the victim's skull had been crushed by a blunt tool, which resulted in a brain hemorrhage. As of now, there is no clear motive for the murder.

35.   The victim <u>is</u> a thirty-five-year-old who had been apparently <u>bludgeoned</u> to death and dumped in the <u>ocean late</u> last night. *(Rigorous)*

   A. was
   B. bludgoned
   C. ocean: late
   D. No change is necessary.

Answer: A. was
The past tense *was* is needed to maintain consistency. Option B creates a misspelling. Option C incorrectly uses a colon when none is needed.

36. The discovery of a body at Paris Point <u>marina</u> in Boca Raton shocked the <u>residents</u> of Palmetto Pines, a luxury <u>condominium</u> complex located next door to the marina.
(Rigorous)

    A. Marina
    B. residence
    C. condominnium
    D. No change is necessary.

Answer: A. Marina
Marina is a name that needs to be capitalized. Options B and C create misspellings.

37. Deputies found five bullets on the sidewalk and some <u>blood,</u> along with a steel pipe that is <u>assumed</u> <u>to be</u> the murder weapon.
(Rigorous)

    A. blood;
    B. assuming
    C. to have been
    D. No change is necessary.

Answer: C. to have been
The past tense *to have been* is needed to maintain consistency. Option A incorrectly uses a semicolon, instead of a comma. Option B uses the wrong form of the verb *assumed.*

38. Many <u>neighbors</u> reported terrible screams, <u>gunshots: as</u> well as the sound of a car, backfiring <u>loudly</u> to Boca Raton Police shortly after midnight.
(Average)

    A. nieghbors
    B. gunshots, as
    C. loud
    D. No change is necessary.

Answer: B. gunshots, as
Option B correctly uses a comma, not a colon to separate the items. Option A creates a misspelling. Option C incorrectly changes the adverb into an adjective.

39. The woman <u>had</u> been spotted in the lobby of Palmetto Pines around ten <u>thirty,</u> along with an older <u>man, estimated</u> to be in his fifties, and a younger man in his late twenties.
(Average)

A. has
B. thirty;
C. man estimated
D. No change is necessary.

Answer: C. man estimated
A comma is not needed to separate the item because *an older man estimated to be in his fifties* is one complete fragment. Option A incorrectly uses the present tense *has* instead of the past tense *had*. Option B incorrectly uses a colon when a comma is needed.

40. "Apparently, the victim had been driven to the complex by the older man and was seen arguing with him when the younger man intervened," said <u>Sheriff Fred Adams, "all</u> three of them left the building together and walked to the marina, where gunshots rang out an hour later."
(Rigorous)

A. sheriff Fred Adams, "all
B. sheriff Fred Adams, "All
C. Sheriff Fred Adams. "All
D. No change is necessary.

Answer: C. Sheriff Fred Adams. "All
The quote's source comes in the middle of two independent clauses, so a period should follow *Adams*. Option A is incorrect because titles, when they come before a name, must be capitalized. Punctuation is also faulty. Option B is incorrect because the word *Adams* ends a sentence; a comma is not strong enough to support two sentences.

TExES PEDAGOGY AND PROFESSIONAL RESPONSIBILITIES EC-4 100

Directions: Read each item and select the best response.

1. **What are critical elements of instructional process?**

   A. Content, goals, teacher needs
   B. Means of getting money to regulate instruction
   C. Content, materials, activities, goals, learner needs
   D. Materials, definitions, assignments

2. **What would improve planning for instruction?**

   A. Describe the role of the teacher and student
   B. Evaluate the outcomes of instruction
   C. Rearrange the order of activities
   D. Give outside assignments

3. **When are students more likely to understand complex ideas?**

   A. If they do outside research before coming to class
   B. Later when they write out the definitions of complex words
   C. When they attend a lecture on the subject
   D. When they are clearly defined by the teacher and are given examples and non-examples of the concept

4. **What is one component of the instructional planning model that must be given careful evaluation?**

   A. Students' prior knowledge and skills
   B. The script the teacher will use in instruction
   C. Future lesson plans
   D. Parent participation

5. **When is utilization of instructional materials most effective?**

   A. When the activities are sequenced
   B. When the materials are prepared ahead of time
   C. When the students choose the pages to work on
   D. When the students create the instructional materials

6. **What should a teacher do when students have not responded well to an instructional activity?**

   A. Reevaluate learner needs
   B. Request administrative help
   C. Continue with the activity another day
   D. Assign homework on the concept

7. **How can student misconduct be redirected at times?**

A. The teacher threatens the students
B. The teacher assigns detention to the whole class
C. The teacher stops the activity and stares at the students
D. The teacher effectively handles changing from one activity to another

8. **What is one way of effectively managing student conduct?**

A. State expectations about behavior
B. Let students discipline their peers
C. Let minor infractions of the rules go unnoticed
D. Increase disapproving remarks

9. **Which of the following increases appropriate behavior more than 80%?**

A. Monitoring the halls
B. Having class rules
C. Having class rules, giving feedback, and having individual consequences
D. Having class rules, and giving feedback

10. **What developmental patterns should a professional teacher assess to meet the needs of the student?**

A. Academic, regional, and family background
B. Social, physical, academic
C. Academic, physical, and family background
D. Physical, family, ethnic background

11. **According to Piaget, what stage is characterized by the ability to think abstractly and to use logic?**

A. Concrete operations
B. Pre-operational
C. Formal operations
D. Conservative operational

12. **At approximately what age is the average child able to define abstract terms such as honesty and justice?**

A. 10-12 years old
B. 4-6 years old
C. 14-16 years old
D. 6-8 years old

13. **Johnny, a middle-schooler, comes to class, uncharacteristically tired, distracted, withdrawn, sullen, and cries easily. What should be the teacher's first response?**

A. Send him to the office to sit
B. Call his parents
C. Ask him what is wrong
D. Ignore his behavior

14. **Sam, a 10-year-old fifth grader, has suddenly started to stutter when speaking. What is the most likely speech problem?**

   A. A genetic defect
   B. A new habit
   C. Evidence of an emotional conflict
   D. An attention-getting device

15. **Andy shows up to class abusive and irritable. He is often late, sleeps in class, sometimes slurs his speech, and has an odor of drinking. What is the first intervention to take?**

   A. Confront him, relying on a trusting relationship you think you have
   B. Do a lesson on alcohol abuse, making an example of him
   C. Do nothing, it is better to err on the side of failing to identify substance abuse
   D. Call administration, avoid conflict, and supervise others carefully

16. **A 16 year-old girl who has been looking sad writes an essay in which the main protagonist commits suicide. You overhear her talking about suicide. What do you do?**

   A. Report this immediately to school administration, talk to the girl, letting her know you will talk to her parents about it
   B. Report this immediately to authorities
   C. Report this immediately to school administration. Make your own report to authorities if required by protocol in your school. Do nothing else.
   D. Just give the child some extra attention, as it may just be that's all she's looking for

17. You are leading a substance abuse discussion for health class. The students present their belief that marijuana is not harmful to their health. What set of data would refute their claim?

A. It is more carcinogenic than nicotine, lowers resistance to infection, worsens acne, and damages brain cells
B. It damages brain cells, causes behavior changes in prenatally exposed infants, leads to other drug abuse, and causes short-term memory loss
C. It lowers tolerance for frustration, causes eye damage, increases paranoia, and lowers resistance to infection
D. It leads to abusing alcohol, lowers white blood cell count, reduces fertility, and causes gout

18. Jeanne, a bright, attentive student is in first hour English. She is quiet, but very alert, often visually scanning the room in random patterns. Her pupils are dilated and she has a slight but noticeable tremor in her hands. She fails to note a cue given from her teacher. At odd moments she will act as if responding to stimuli that aren't there by suddenly changing her gaze. When spoken to directly, she has a limited response, but her teacher has a sense she is not herself. What should the teacher do?

A. Ask the student if she is all right, then let it go, as there are not enough signals to be alarmed
B. Meet with the student after class to get more information before making a referral
C. Send the student to the office to see the health nurse
D. Quietly call for administration, remain calm and be careful not to alarm the class

19. Marcus is a first grade boy of good developmental attainment. His learning progress is good the first half of the year. He shows no indicators of emotional distress. After the holiday break, he returns much changed. He is quieter, sullen even, tending to play alone. He has moments of tearfulness, sometimes almost without cause. He avoids contact with adults as often as he can. Even play with his friends has become limited. He has episodes of wetting not seen before, and often wants to sleep in school. What approach is appropriate for this sudden change in behavior?

A. Give him some time to adjust. The holiday break was probably too much fun to come back to school from
B. Report this change immediately to administration. Do not call the parents until administration decides a course of action
C. Document his daily behavior carefully as soon as you notice such a change, report to administration the next month or so in a meeting
D. Make a courtesy call to the parents to let them know he is not acting like himself, being sure to tell them he is not making trouble for others

20. What have recent studies regarding effective teachers concluded?

A. Effective teachers let students establish rules
B. Effective teachers establish routines by the sixth week of school
C. Effective teachers state their own policies and establish consistent class rules and procedures on the first day of class
D. Effective teachers establish flexible routines

21. To maintain the flow of events in the classroom, what should an effective teacher do?

A. Work only in small groups
B. Use only whole class activities
C. Direct attention to content, rather than focusing the class on misbehavior
D. Follow lectures with written assignments

22. Why is it important for a teacher to pose a question before calling on students to answer?

A. It helps manage student conduct
B. It keeps the students as a group focused on the class work
C. It allows students time to collaborate
D. It gives the teacher time to walk among the students

23. **Which statement is an example of specific praise?**

A. "John, you are the only person in class not paying attention"
B. "William, I thought we agreed that you would turn in all of your homework"
C. "Robert, you did a good job staying in line. See how it helped us get to music class on time?"
D. "Class, you did a great job cleaning up the art room"

24. **What is one way a teacher can supplement verbal praise?**

A. Help students evaluate their own performance and supply self-reinforcement
B. Give verbal praise more frequently
C. Give tangible rewards such as stickers or treats
D. Have students practice giving verbal praise

25. **Reducing off task time and maximizing the amount of time students spend attending to academic tasks is closely related to which of the following?**

A. Using whole class instruction only
B. Business-like behaviors of the teacher
C. Dealing only with major teaching functions
D. Giving students a maximum of two minutes to come to order

26. **The concept of efficient use of time includes which of the following?**

A. Daily review, seatwork, and recitation of concepts
B. Lesson initiation, transition, and comprehension check
C. Review, test, review
D. Punctuality, management transition, and wait time avoidance

27. **What steps are important in the review of subject matter in the classroom?**

A. A lesson-initiating review, topic, and a lesson-end review
B. A preview of the subject matter, an in-depth discussion, and a lesson-end review
C. A rehearsal of the subject matter and a topic summary within the lesson
D. A short paragraph synopsis of the previous day's lesson and a written review at the end of the lesson

28. **What is a sample of an academic transition signal?**

A. "How do clouds form?"
B. "Today we are going to study clouds."
C. "We have completed today's lesson."
D. "That completes the description of cumulus clouds. Now we will look at the description of cirrus clouds."

29. **What is an example of a low order question?**

A. "Why is it important to recycle items in your home?"
B. "Compare how glass and plastics are recycled"
C. "What items do we recycle in our county?"
D. "Explain the importance of recycling in our county"

30. **The teacher states that the lesson the students will be engaged in will consist of a review of the material from the previous day, a demonstration of the scientific principles of an electronic circuit, and small group work on setting up an electronic circuit. What has the teacher demonstrated?**

A. The importance of reviewing
B. Giving the general framework for the lesson to facilitate learning
C. Giving students the opportunity to leave if they are not interested in the lesson
D. Providing momentum for the lesson

31. **Wait-time has what effect?**

A. Gives structure to the class discourse
B. Fewer chain and low level questions are asked with more high-level questions included
C. Gives the students time to evaluate the response
D. Gives the opportunity for in-depth discussion about the topic

32. **What is one benefit of amplifying a student's response?**

A. It helps the student develop a positive self-image
B. It is helpful to other students who are in the process of learning the reasoning or steps in answering the question
C. It allows the teacher to cover more content
D. It helps to keep the information organized

33. **A study by Darch and Gersten that examined the effects of positive feedback on the reading performance of seven and eight-year old learning disabled students found which result?**

A. Students exhibited more self-esteem
B. Students exhibited more on-task behavior
C. Students were willing to answer more questions
D. Students worked better in small groups

34. **When is optimal benefit reached when handling an incorrect student response?**

   A. When specific praise is used
   B. When the other students are allowed to correct that student
   C. When the student is redirected to a better problem solving approach
   D. When the teacher asks simple questions, provides cues to clarify, or gives assistance for working out the correct response

35. **What are the two ways concepts can be taught?**

   A. Factually and interpretively
   B. Inductively and deductively
   C. Conceptually and inductively
   D. Analytically and facilitatively

36. **Using pro-active expressions and repetition has what effect on students?**

   A. Helps student become aware of important elements of content
   B. Helps students develop positive self-esteem
   C. Helps students tolerate the lecture format of instruction
   D. Helps students to complete homework correctly

37. **How can the teacher help students become more work oriented and less disruptive?**

   A. Seek their input for content instruction
   B. Challenge the students with a task and show genuine enthusiasm for it
   C. Use behavior modification techniques with all students
   D. Make sure lesson plans are complete for the week

38. **What is an effective way to prepare students for testing?**

   A. Minimize the importance of the test
   B. Orient the students to the test, telling them of the purpose, how the results will be used and how it is relevant to them
   C. Use the same format for every test given
   D. Have them construct an outline to study from

39. **How will students have a fair chance to demonstrate what they know on a test?**

   A. The examiner has strictly enforced rules for taking the test
   B. The examiner provides a comfortable setting free of distractions and positively encourages the students
   C. The examiner provides frequent stretch breaks to the students
   D. The examiner stresses the importance of the test to the overall grade

40. **What is an example of formative feedback?**

   A. The results of an intelligence test
   B. Correcting the tests in small groups
   C. Verbal behavior that expresses approval of a student response to a test item
   D. Scheduling a discussion prior to the test

41. **How could a KWL chart be used in instruction?**

   A. To motivate students to do a research paper
   B. To assess prior knowledge of the students
   C. To assist in teaching skills
   D. To put events in sequential order

42. **How can the teacher establish a positive climate in the classroom?**

   A. Help students see the unique contributions of individual differences
   B. Use whole group instruction for all content areas
   C. Help students divide into cooperative groups based on ability
   D. Eliminate teaching strategies that allow students to make choices

43. **How can students use a computer desktop publishing center?**

   A. To set up a classroom budget
   B. To create student made books
   C. To design a research project
   D. To create a classroom behavior management system

44. **Which of the following is an example of a synthesis question according to Bloom's taxonomy?**

   A. "What is the definition of_____?"
   B. "Compare_____ to _____."
   C. "Match column A to column B."
   D. "Propose an alternative to_____."

45. **What is a good strategy for teaching ethnically diverse students?**

   A. Don't focus on the students' culture
   B. Expect them to assimilate easily into your classroom
   C. Imitate their speech patterns
   D. Include ethnic studies in the curriculum

46. **How many stages of intellectual development does Piaget define?**

   A. Two
   B. Four
   C. Six
   D. Eight

47. **What is the most significant development emerging in children at age two?**

A. Immune system develops
B. Socialization occurs
C. Language develops
D. Perception develops

48. **According to Piaget, when does the development of symbolic functioning and language take place?**

A. Concrete operations stage
B. Formal operations stage
C. Sensorimotor stage
D. Preoperational stage

49. **What is the learning theorist's view of language acquisition?**

A. Language is shaped by the reinforcement children receive from their caretakers
B. Language is the result of innate biological mechanisms
C. Language results spontaneously
D. Language is developed through systematic instruction

50. **Bobby, a nine year-old, has been caught stealing frequently in the classroom. What might be a factor contributing to this behavior?**

A. Need for the items stolen
B. Serious emotional disturbance
C. Desire to experiment
D. A normal stage of development

51. **What does the validity of a test refer to?**

A. Its consistency
B. Its usefulness
C. Its accuracy
D. The degree of true scores it provides

52. **What is the best definition for an achievement test?**

A. It measures mechanical and practical abilities
B. It measures broad areas of knowledge that are the result of cumulative learning experiences
C. It measures the ability to learn to perform a task
D. It measures performance related to specific, recently acquired information

53. **Which of the following is an accurate description of ESL students?**

A. Remedial students
B. Exceptional education students
C. Are not a homogeneous group
D. Feel confident in communicating in English when with their peers

54. **What is an effective way to help a non-English speaking student succeed in class?**

A. Refer the child to a specialist
B. Maintain an encouraging, success-oriented atmosphere
C. Help them assimilate by making them use English exclusively
D. Help them cope with the content materials you presently use

55. **What should be considered when evaluating textbooks for content?**

A. Type of print used
B. Number of photos used
C. Free of cultural stereotyping
D. Outlines at the beginning of each chapter

56. **How can text be modified for low-level ESL students?**

A. Add visuals and illustrations
B. Let students write definitions
C. Change text to a narrative form
D. Have students write details out from the text

57. **Which of the following is considered a study skill?**

A. Using graphs, tables, and maps
B. Using a desk-top publishing program
C. Explaining important vocabulary words
D. Asking for clarification

58. **When using a kinesthetic approach, what would be an appropriate activity?**

A. List
B. Match
C. Define
D. Debate

59. **Etienne is an ESL student. He has begun to engage in conversation which produces a connected narrative. What developmental stage for second language acquisition is he in?**

A. Early production
B. Speech emergence
C. Preproduction
D. Intermediate fluency

60. **What is a roadblock to second language learning?**

A. Students are forced to speak
B. Students speak only when ready
C. Mistakes are considered a part of learning
D. The focus is on oral communication

61. **What do cooperative learning methods all have in common?**

A. Philosophy
B. Cooperative task/cooperative reward structures
C. Student roles and communication
D. Teacher roles

62. **Who developed the theory of multiple intelligences?**

    A. Bruner
    B. Gardner
    C. Kagan
    D. Cooper

63. **According to research, what can be a result of specific teacher actions on behavior?**

    A. Increase in student misconduct
    B. Increase in the number of referrals
    C. Decrease in student participation
    D. Decrease in student retentions

64. **What is the definition of proactive classroom management?**

    A. Management that is constantly changing
    B. Management that is downplayed
    C. Management that gives clear and explicit instructions and rewards compliance
    D. Management that is designed by the students

65. **What might be a result if the teacher is distracted by some unrelated event in the instruction?**

    A. Students will leave the class
    B. Students will understand the importance of class rules
    C. Students will stay on-task longer
    D. Students will lose the momentum of the lesson

66. **Why is praise for compliance important in classroom management?**

    A. Students will continue deviant behavior
    B. Desirable conduct will be repeated
    C. It reflects simplicity and warmth
    D. Students will fulfill obligations

67. **What is an effective amount of "wait time"?**

    A. 1 second
    B. 5 seconds
    C. 15 seconds
    D. 10 seconds

68. **Mr. Perez has the pictures and maps ready for his lesson. The movie is set up to go, and he tested the operation of the machine before the class came in. What is this an example of?**

    A. Controlled interruptions
    B. Housekeeping
    C. Punctuality
    D. Management transition

69. **How are standardized tests useful in assessment?**

   A. For teacher evaluation
   B. For evaluation of the administration
   C. For comparison from school to school
   D. For comparison to the population on which the test was normed

70. **Ms. Smith says, "Yes, exactly what do you mean by 'It was the author's intention to mislead you.'" What does this illustrate?**

   A. Digression
   B. Restates response
   C. Probes a response
   D. Amplifies a response

71. **What is perhaps the most controversial issue in developmental psychology?**

   A. Interactionism
   B. Nature vs. nurture
   C. Relevance of IQ scores
   D. Change vs. external events

72. **A child exhibits the following symptoms: a lack of emotional responsivity, indifference to physical contact, abnormal social play, and abnormal speech. What is the likely diagnosis for this child?**

   A. Separation anxiety
   B. Mental retardation
   C. Autism
   D. Hypochondria

73. **What is not a way that teachers show acceptance and give value to a student response?**

   A. Acknowledging
   B. Correcting
   C. Discussing
   D. Amplifying

74. **What is teacher with-it-ness?**

   A. Having adequate knowledge of subject matter
   B. A skill that must be mastered to attain certification
   C. Understanding the current fads and trends that affect students
   D. Attending to two tasks at once

75. **What should the teacher do when a student is tapping a pencil on the desk during a lecture?**

   A. Stop the lesson and correct the student as an example to other students
   B. Walk over to the student and quietly touch the pencil as a signal for the student to stop
   C. Announce to the class that everyone should remember to remain quiet during the lecture
   D. Ignore the student, hoping he or she will stop

SAMPLE CONSTRUCTED RESPONSE #1

Use the following scenario to complete the exercise:

In an age of accountability for student learning, many educators assume that sticking to standards and ensuring that each standard is covered explicitly is the safest and most prudent thing to do. However, there are still many educators that believe that standards can be covered, perhaps in a non-linear fashion, by engaging students in academic and cross-curricular projects. Those who believe that project-based instruction is more valuable suggest that students will enjoy their learning more and will still learn many important academic standards in the process. Those who believe that standards-driven learning is more valuable might argue that it is unfair to students to not cover each and every area that they will be tested on. They might also suggest that teaching standards in a linear fashion will provide greater clarity for students.

Exercise
In a response written for an audience of teachers, use your knowledge of learners and the learning environment to analyze and discuss the issue of standards-driven and project-based teaching.

SAMPLE CONSTRUCTED RESPONSE #2

Use the following scenario to complete the exercise:

LEARNING GOAL: Students will learn and apply new information through the use of hands-on activities.

Exercise
In a written response for an audience of teachers, identify a grade/age level and subject area for which you are prepared to teach. Then use your knowledge of instruction and assessment to describe a "hands-on" activity or lesson that would help students to learn and apply new information.

SAMPLE CONSTRUCTED RESPONSE #3

Use the following scenario to complete the exercise:

Scenario
Half-way through the school year, a week after semester report cards are sent home, you get an email from a student's parent complaining that you gave her son low grades for no good reason. She suggests that she has heard nothing but complaints about your teaching and that if you were a better teacher, her son would not have such low grades. She wants to (a) meet with you and the principal together, (b) examine other students' grades to see how her son's grades compare, and (c) have you put together extra credit work so that her son can raise her grade.

Exercise

In a written response to an audience of educators, use your knowledge of the professional environment to:

- Identify the important issues at stake in this scenario.
- Describe a plan of action you would take to remedy this problem.
- Explain why your plan would be effective in resolving the issue.

SAMPLE EXTENDED ESSAY RESPONSE

Goal: Understand various instructional approaches and use this knowledge to facilitate student learning.

Examples of Teaching Objectives

Analyzing the uses, benefits, or limitations of a specific instructional approach (e.g., direct instruction, cooperative learning, interdisciplinary instruction, exploration, discovery learning, independent study, lectures, hands-on activities, peer tutoring, technology-based approach, various discussion methods such as guided discussion, various questioning methods) in relation to given purposes and learners.

Recognizing appropriate strategies for varying the role of the teacher (e.g., working with students as instructor, facilitator, observer; working with other adults in the classroom) in relation to the situation and the instructional approach used.

Comparing instructional approaches in terms of teacher and student responsibilities, expected student outcomes, usefulness for achieving instructional purposes, etc.

Exercise

In an essay written for a group of educators, frame your response by identifying a grade level and/or subject area for which you are prepared to teach; then:

- Explain the importance of using a variety of instructional approaches so that all students can learn and master the standards.
- Describe two strategies to meet this goal.
- Explain why the strategies you have chosen would be effective.

Be sure to specify a grade level/subject area in your essay, and frame your ideas so that an educator at your level will be able to understand the basis for your response.

Answer Key

1.	C	39.	B
2.	B	40.	C
3.	D	41.	B
4.	A	42.	A
5.	A	43.	B
6.	A	44.	D
7.	D	45.	D
8.	A	46.	B
9.	C	47.	C
10.	B	48.	D
11.	C	49.	A
12.	A	50.	B
13.	C	51.	B
14.	C	52.	B
15.	D	53.	C
16.	C	54.	B
17.	B	55.	C
18.	D	56.	A
19.	B	57.	A
20.	C	58.	B
21.	C	59.	D
22.	B	60.	A
23.	C	61.	B
24.	A	62.	B
25.	B	63.	A
26.	D	64.	C
27.	A	65.	D
28.	D	66.	B
29.	C	67.	B
30.	B	68.	B
31.	B	69.	D
32.	B	70.	C
33.	B	71.	B
34.	C	72.	C
35.	B	73.	B
36.	A	74.	D
37.	B	75.	B
38.	B		

PEDAGOGY AND PROFESSIONAL RESPONSIBILITIES RATIONALES

Directions: Read each item and select the best response.

1. **What are critical elements of instructional process?**

    A. Content, goals, teacher needs
    B. Means of getting money to regulate instruction
    C. Content, materials, activities, goals, learner needs
    D. Materials, definitions, assignments

Answer: C. Content, materials, activities, goals, learner needs
Goal-setting is a vital component of the instructional process. The teacher will, of course, have overall goals for her class, both short-term and long-term. However, perhaps even more important than that is the setting of goals that take into account the individual learner's needs, background, and stage of development. Making an educational program child-centered involves building on the natural curiosity children bring to school, and asking children what they want to learn. Student-centered classrooms contain not only textbooks, workbooks, and literature but also rely heavily on a variety of audiovisual equipment and computers. There are tape recorders, language masters, filmstrip projectors, and laser disc players to help meet the learning styles of the students. Planning for instructional activities entails identification or selection of the activities the teacher and students will engage in during a period of instruction.

2. **What would improve planning for instruction?**

    A. Describe the role of the teacher and student
    B. Evaluate the outcomes of instruction
    C. Rearrange the order of activities
    D. Give outside assignments

Answer: B. Evaluate the outcomes of instruction
Important as it is to plan content, materials, activities, and goals taking into account learner needs and to base what goes on in the classroom on the results of that planning, it makes no difference if students are not able to demonstrate improvement in the skills being taught. An important part of the planning process is for the teacher to constantly adapt all aspects of the curriculum to what is actually happening in the classroom. Planning frequently misses the mark or fails to allow for unexpected factors. Evaluating the outcomes of instruction regularly and making adjustments accordingly will have a positive impact on the overall success of a teaching methodology.

3. **When are students more likely to understand complex ideas?**

   A. If they do outside research before coming to class
   B. Later when they write out the definitions of complex words
   C. When they attend a lecture on the subject
   D. When they are clearly defined by the teacher and are given examples and non-examples of the concept

Answer: D. When they are clearly defined by the teacher and are given examples and non-examples of the concept
Several studies have been carried out to determine the effectiveness of giving examples as well as the difference in effectiveness of various types of examples. It was found conclusively that the most effective method of concept presentation included giving a definition along with examples and non-examples and also providing an explanation of them. These same studies indicate that boring examples were just as effective as interesting examples in promoting learning. Additional studies have been conducted to determine the most effective number of examples that will result in maximum student learning. These studies concluded that a few thoughtfully selected examples are just as effective as many examples. It was determined that the actual number of examples necessary to promote student learning was relative to the learning characteristics of the learners. It was again ascertained that learning is facilitated when examples are provided along with the definition.

4. **What is one component of the instructional planning model that must be given careful evaluation?**

   A. Students' prior knowledge and skills
   B. The script the teacher will use in instruction
   C. Future lesson plans
   D. Parent participation

Answer: A. Students' prior knowledge and skills
The teacher will, of course, have certain expectations regarding where the students will be physically and intellectually when he/she plans for a new class. However, there will be wide variations in the actual classroom. If he/she doesn't make the extra effort to understand where there are deficiencies and where there are strengths in the individual students, the planning will probably miss the mark, at least for some members of the class. This can be obtained through a review of student records, by observation, and by testing.

5. **When is utilization of instructional materials most effective?**

   A. When the activities are sequenced
   B. When the materials are prepared ahead of time
   C. When the students choose the pages to work on
   D. When the students create the instructional materials

Answer: A. When the activities are sequenced

Most assignments will require more than one educational principle. It is helpful to explain to students the proper order in which these principles must be applied to complete the assignment successfully. Subsequently, students should also be informed of the nature of the assignment (i.e., cooperative learning, group project, individual assignment, etc). This is often done at the start of the assignment.

6. **What should a teacher do when students have not responded well to an instructional activity?**

   A. Reevaluate learner needs
   B. Request administrative help
   C. Continue with the activity another day
   D. Assign homework on the concept

Answer: A. Reevaluate learner needs

The value of teacher observations cannot be underestimated. It is through the use of observations that the teacher is able to informally assess the needs of the students during instruction. These observations will drive the lesson and determine the direction that the lesson will take based on student activity and behavior. After a lesson is carefully planned, teacher observation is the single most important component of an instructional presentation. If the teacher observes that a particular student is not on-task, she will change the method of instruction accordingly. She may change from a teacher-directed approach to a more interactive approach. Questioning will increase in order to increase the participation of the students. If appropriate, the teacher will introduce manipulative materials to the lesson. In addition, teachers may switch to a cooperative group activity, thereby removing the responsibility of instruction from the teacher and putting it on the students.

7. **How can student misconduct be redirected at times?**

   A. The teacher threatens the students
   B. The teacher assigns detention to the whole class
   C. The teacher stops the activity and stares at the students
   D. The teacher effectively handles changing from one activity to another

Answer: D. The teacher effectively handles changing from one activity to another
Appropriate verbal techniques include a soft, non-threatening voice void of undue roughness, anger, or impatience regardless of whether the teacher is instructing, providing student alerts, or giving a behavior reprimand. Verbal techniques that may be effective in modifying student behavior include simply stating the student's name, explaining briefly and succinctly what the student is doing that is inappropriate and what the student should be doing. Verbal techniques for reinforcing behavior include both encouragement and praise delivered by the teacher. In addition, for verbal techniques to positively affect student behavior and learning, the teacher must give clear, concise directives while implying her warmth toward the students.

8. **What is one way of effectively managing student conduct?**

   A. State expectations about behavior
   B. Let students discipline their peers
   C. Let minor infractions of the rules go unnoticed
   D. Increase disapproving remarks

Answer: A. State expectations about behavior
The effective teacher demonstrates awareness of what the entire class is doing and is in control of the behavior of all students even when the teacher is working with only a small group of the children. In an attempt to prevent student misbehaviors the teacher makes clear, concise statements about what is happening in the classroom directing attention to content and the students' accountability for their work rather than focusing the class on the misbehavior. It is also effective for the teacher to make a positive statement about the appropriate behavior that is observed. If deviant behavior does occur, the effective teacher will specify who the deviant is, what he or she is doing wrong, and why this is unacceptable conduct or what the proper conduct would be. This can be a difficult task to accomplish as the teacher must maintain academic focus and flow while addressing and desisting misbehavior. The teacher must make clear, brief statements about the expectations without raising his/her voice and without disrupting instruction.

9. **Which of the following increases appropriate behavior more than 80%?**

    A. Monitoring the halls
    B. Having class rules
    C. Having class rules, giving feedback, and having individual consequences
    D. Having class rules, and giving feedback

Answer: C. Having class rules, giving feedback, and having individual consequences

Clear, consistent class rules go a long way to preventing inappropriate behavior. Effective teachers give immediate feedback to students regarding their behavior or misbehavior. If there are consequences, they should be as close as possible to the outside world, especially for adolescents. Consistency, especially with adolescents, reduces the occurrence of power struggles and teaches them that predictable consequences follow for their choice of actions.

10. **What developmental patterns should a professional teacher assess to meet the needs of the student?**

    A. Academic, regional, and family background
    B. Social, physical, academic
    C. Academic, physical, and family background
    D. Physical, family, ethnic background

Answer: B. Social, physical, academic

The effective teacher applies knowledge of physical, social, and academic developmental patterns and of individual differences, to meet the instructional needs of all students in the classroom. The most important premise of child development is that all domains of development (physical, social, and academic) are integrated. The teacher has a broad knowledge and thorough understanding of the development that typically occurs during the students' current period of life. More importantly, the teacher understands how children learn best during each period of development. An examination of the student's file coupled with ongoing evaluation assures a successful educational experience for both teacher and students.

11. **According to Piaget, what stage is characterized by the ability to think abstractly and to use logic?**

   A. Concrete operations
   B. Pre-operational
   C. Formal operations
   D. Conservative operational

Answer: C. Formal operations
The four development stages are described in Piaget's theory as follows:

   1. Sensorimotor stage: from birth to age 2 years (children experience the world through movement and senses)
   2. Preoperational stage: from ages 2 to 7 (acquisition of motor skills)
   3. Concrete operational stage: from ages 7 to 11 (children begin to think logically about concrete events)
   4. Formal operational stage: after age 11 (development of abstract reasoning)

These chronological periods are approximate and, in light of the fact that studies have demonstrated great variation between children, cannot be seem as rigid norms. Furthermore, these stages occur at different ages, depending upon the domain of knowledge under consideration. The ages normally given for the stages reflect when each stage tends to predominate even though one might elicit examples of two, three, or even all four stages of thinking at the same time from one individual, depending upon the domain of knowledge and the means used to elicit it.

12. **At approximately what age is the average child able to define abstract terms such as honesty and justice?**

   A. 10-12 years old
   B. 4-6 years old
   C. 14-16 years old
   D. 6-8 years old

Answer: A. 10-12 years old
The usual age for the fourth stage (the formal operational stage) as described by Piaget is from 10 to 12 years old. It is in this stage that children begin to be able to define abstract terms.

13. **Johnny, a middle-schooler, comes to class, uncharacteristically tired, distracted, withdrawn, sullen, and cries easily. What should be the teacher's first response?**

   A. Send him to the office to sit
   B. Call his parents
   C. Ask him what is wrong
   D. Ignore his behavior

Answer: C. Ask him what is wrong
If a teacher has developed a trusting relationship with a child, the reasons for the child's behavior may come out. It might be that the child needs to tell someone what is going on and is seeking a confidant, and a trusted teacher can intervene. If the child is unwilling to talk to the teacher about what is going on, the next step is to contact the parents, who may or may not be willing to explain why the child is the way he/she is. If they simply do not know, then it's time to add a professional physician or counselor to the mix.

14. **Sam, a 10-year-old fifth grader, has suddenly started to stutter when speaking. What is the most likely speech problem?**

   A. A genetic defect
   B. A new habit
   C. Evidence of an emotional conflict
   D. An attention-getting device

Answer: C. Evidence of an emotional conflict
Much of what constitutes stuttering cannot be observed by the listener; this includes such things as sound and word fears, situational fears, anxiety, tension, shame, and a feeling of loss of control during speech. The emotional state of the individual who stutters often constitutes the most difficult aspect of the disorder. If a student suddenly begins to stutter, an investigation into what is happening in the child's life should be initiated.

15. **Andy shows up to class abusive and irritable. He is often late, sleeps in class, sometimes slurs his speech, and has an odor of drinking. What is the first intervention to take?**

   A. Confront him, relying on a trusting relationship you think you have
   B. Do a lesson on alcohol abuse, making an example of him
   C. Do nothing, it is better to err on the side of failing to identify substance abuse
   D. Call administration, avoid conflict, and supervise others carefully

Answer: D. Call administration, avoid conflict, and supervise others carefully
Educators are not only likely to, but often do face students who are high on something. Of course, they are not only a hazard to their own safety and those of others, but their ability to be productive learners is greatly diminished, if not non-existent. They show up instead of skip, because it's not always easy or practical for them to spend the day away from home, but not in school. Unless they can stay inside they are at risk of being picked up for truancy. Some enjoy being high in school, getting a sense of satisfaction by putting something over on the system. Some just don't take drug use seriously enough to think usage at school might be inappropriate. The first responsibility of the teacher is to assure the safety of all of the children. Avoiding conflict with the student who is high and obtaining help from administration is the best course of action.

16. **A 16 year-old girl who has been looking sad writes an essay in which the main protagonist commits suicide. You overhear her talking about suicide. What do you do?**

   A. Report this immediately to school administration, talk to the girl, letting her know you will talk to her parents about it
   B. Report this immediately to authorities
   C. Report this immediately to school administration. Make your own report to authorities if required by protocol in your school. Do nothing else.
   D. Just give the child some extra attention, as it may just be that's all she's looking for

Answer: C. Report this immediately to school administration. Make your own report to authorities if required by protocol in your school. Do nothing else.
A child who is suicidal is beyond any help that can be offered in a classroom. The first step is to report the situation to administration. If your school protocol calls for it, the situation should also be reported to authorities.

17. **You are leading a substance abuse discussion for health class. The students present their belief that marijuana is not harmful to their health. What set of data would refute their claim?**

   A. It is more carcinogenic than nicotine, lowers resistance to infection, worsens acne, and damages brain cells
   B. It damages brain cells, causes behavior changes in prenatally exposed infants, leads to other drug abuse, and causes short-term memory loss
   C. It lowers tolerance for frustration, causes eye damage, increases paranoia, and lowers resistance to infection
   D. It leads to abusing alcohol, lowers white blood cell count, reduces fertility, and causes gout

Answer: B. It damages brain cells, causes behavior changes in prenatally exposed infants, leads to other drug abuse, and causes short-term memory loss
The student tending toward the use of drugs and /or alcohol will exhibit losses in social and academic functional levels that were previously attained. He may begin to experiment with substances. The adage, "Pot makes a smart kid average and an average kid dumb," is right on the mark. There exist not a few families where pot smoking is a known habit of the parents. The children start their habit by stealing from the parents, making it almost impossible to convince the child that drugs and alcohol are not good for them. Parental use is hampering national efforts to clean up America. The school may be the only source for the real information that children need in order to make intelligent choices about drug use. It's important to remember that if children start using drugs early, it will interfere with their accomplishing developmental tasks and will likely lead to a lifetime of addiction.

18. Jeanne, a bright, attentive student is in first hour English. She is quiet, but very alert, often visually scanning the room in random patterns. Her pupils are dilated and she has a slight but noticeable tremor in her hands. She fails to note a cue given from her teacher. At odd moments she will act as if responding to stimuli that aren't there by suddenly changing her gaze. When spoken to directly, she has a limited response, but her teacher has a sense she is not herself. What should the teacher do?

A. Ask the student if she is all right, then let it go, as there are not enough signals to be alarmed
B. Meet with the student after class to get more information before making a referral
C. Send the student to the office to see the health nurse
D. Quietly call for administration, remain calm and be careful not to alarm the class

Answer: D. Quietly call for administration, remain calm and be careful not to alarm the class

These behaviors are indicative of drug use. The best thing a teacher can do in this case is call for help from administration.

19. **Marcus is a first grade boy of good developmental attainment. His learning progress is good the first half of the year. He shows no indicators of emotional distress. After the holiday break, he returns much changed. He is quieter, sullen even, tending to play alone. He has moments of tearfulness, sometimes almost without cause. He avoids contact with adults as often as he can. Even play with his friends has become limited. He has episodes of wetting not seen before, and often wants to sleep in school. What approach is appropriate for this sudden change in behavior?**

   A. Give him some time to adjust. The holiday break was probably too much fun to come back to school from
   B. Report this change immediately to administration. Do not call the parents until administration decides a course of action
   C. Document his daily behavior carefully as soon as you notice such a change, report to administration the next month or so in a meeting
   D. Make a courtesy call to the parents to let them know he is not acting like himself, being sure to tell them he is not making trouble for others

Answer: B. Report this change immediately to administration. Do not call the parents until administration decides a course of action

Anytime a child's disposition, attitude, or habits change significantly, teachers and parents need to seriously consider the existence of emotional difficulties. Emotional disturbances in childhood are not uncommon and take a variety of forms. Usually these problems show up in the form of uncharacteristic behaviors. Most of the time, children respond favorably to brief treatment programs of psychotherapy. At other times, disturbances may need more intensive therapy and are harder to resolve. All stressful behaviors need to be addressed, and any type of chronic, antisocial behavior needs to be examined as a possible symptom of deep-seated emotional upset. In a case where the change is sudden and dramatic, administration needs to become involved.

20. What have recent studies regarding effective teachers concluded?

A. Effective teachers let students establish rules
B. Effective teachers establish routines by the sixth week of school
C. Effective teachers state their own policies and establish consistent class rules and procedures on the first day of class
D. Effective teachers establish flexible routines

Answer: C. Effective teachers state their own policies and establish consistent class rules and procedures on the first day of class
The teacher can get ahead of the game by stating clearly on the first day of school in her introductory information for the students exactly what the rules are. These should be stated firmly but unemotionally. When one of those rules is broken, he/she can then refer to the rules, rendering enforcement much easier to achieve. It's extremely difficult to achieve goals with students who are out of control. Establishing limits early and consistently enforcing them enhances learning. It is also helpful for the teacher to display prominently the classroom rules. This will serve as a visual reminder of the students' expected behaviors. In a study of classroom management procedures, it was established that the combination of conspicuously displayed rules, frequent verbal references to the rules, and appropriate consequences for appropriate behaviors led to increased levels of on-task behavior.

21. To maintain the flow of events in the classroom, what should an effective teacher do?

A. Work only in small groups
B. Use only whole class activities
C. Direct attention to content, rather than focusing the class on misbehavior
D. Follow lectures with written assignments

Answer: C. Direct attention to content, rather than focusing the class on misbehavior
Students who misbehave often do so to attract attention. Focusing the attention of the misbehaver, as well as the rest of the class, on the real purpose of the classroom sends the message that misbehaving will not be rewarded with class attention to the misbehaver. Engaging students in content by using the various tools available to the creative teacher goes a long way in ensuring a peaceful classroom.

22.   **Why is it important for a teacher to pose a question before calling on students to answer?**

    A. It helps manage student conduct
    B. It keeps the students as a group focused on the class work
    C. It allows students time to collaborate
    D. It gives the teacher time to walk among the students

Answer: B. It keeps the students as a group focused on the class work
It doesn't take much distraction for a class's attention to become diffused. Once this happens, effectively teaching a principle or a skill is very difficult. The teacher should plan presentations that will keep students focused on the lesson. A very useful tool is effective, well-thought-out, pointed questions.

23.   **Which statement is an example of specific praise?**

    A. "John, you are the only person in class not paying attention"
    B. "William, I thought we agreed that you would turn in all of your homework"
    C. "Robert, you did a good job staying in line. See how it helped us get to music class on time?"
    D. "Class, you did a great job cleaning up the art room"

Answer: C. "Robert, you did a good job staying in line. See how it helped us get to music class on time?"
Praise is a powerful tool in obtaining and maintaining order in a classroom. In addition, it is an effective motivator. It is even more effective if the positive results of good behavior are included.

24.   **What is one way a teacher can supplement verbal praise?**

    A. Help students evaluate their own performance and supply self-reinforcement
    B. Give verbal praise more frequently
    C. Give tangible rewards such as stickers or treats
    D. Have students practice giving verbal praise

Answer: A. Help students evaluate their own performance and supply self-reinforcement
While praise is useful in maintaining order in a classroom and in motivating students, it's important for the teacher to remember at all times that one major educational objective is that of preparing students to succeed in the world once the supports of the classroom are gone. Lack of self-esteem is often a barrier to success. An important lesson and skill for students to learn is how to bolster one's own self-esteem and confidence.

25. **Reducing off task time and maximizing the amount of time students spend attending to academic tasks is closely related to which of the following?**

    A. Using whole class instruction only
    B. Business-like behaviors of the teacher
    C. Dealing only with major teaching functions
    D. Giving students a maximum of two minutes to come to order

Answer: B. Business-like behaviors of the teacher
The effective teacher continually evaluates his/her own physical/mental/social/emotional well-being with regard to the students in his/her classroom. There is always the tendency to satisfy social and emotional needs through relationships with the students. A good teacher genuinely likes his/her students, and that's a positive thing. However, if students are not convinced that the teacher's purpose for being there is to get a job done, the atmosphere in the classroom becomes difficult to control. This is the job of the teacher. Maintaining a business-like approach in the classroom yields many positive results. It's a little like a benevolent boss.

26. **The concept of efficient use of time includes which of the following?**

    A. Daily review, seatwork, and recitation of concepts
    B. Lesson initiation, transition, and comprehension check
    C. Review, test, review
    D. Punctuality, management transition, and wait time avoidance

Answer: D. Punctuality, management transition, and wait time avoidance
The "benevolent boss" described in the rationale for question 25 applies here. One who succeeds in managing a business follows these rules; so does the successful teacher.

27. **What steps are important in the review of subject matter in the classroom?**

    A. A lesson-initiating review, topic, and a lesson-end review
    B. A preview of the subject matter, an in-depth discussion, and a lesson-end review
    C. A rehearsal of the subject matter and a topic summary within the lesson
    D. A short paragraph synopsis of the previous day's lesson and a written review at the end of the lesson

Answer: A. A lesson-initiating review, topic, and a lesson-end review
The effective teacher utilizes all three of these together with comprehension checks to make sure the students are processing the information. Lesson-end reviews are restatements (by the teacher or teacher and students) of the content of discussion at the end of a lesson. Subject matter retention increases when lessons include an outline at the beginning of the lesson and a summary at the end of the lesson. This type of structure is utilized in successful classrooms. Moreover, when students know what is coming next, and what is expected of them, they feel more a part of their learning environment and deviant behavior is lessened.

28. **What is a sample of an academic transition signal?**

   A. "How do clouds form?"
   B. "Today we are going to study clouds."
   C. "We have completed today's lesson."
   D. "That completes the description of cumulus clouds. Now we will look at the description of cirrus clouds."

Answer: D. "That completes the description of cumulus clouds. Now we will look at the description of cirrus clouds."
Transitions are language bridges between one topic and another. The teacher should thoughtfully plan transitions when several topics are going to be presented in one lesson to be sure that students are carried along. Without transitions, sometimes students are still focused on a previous topic and are lost in the discussion.

29. **What is an example of a low order question?**

   A. "Why is it important to recycle items in your home?"
   B. "Compare how glass and plastics are recycled"
   C. "What items do we recycle in our county?"
   D. "Explain the importance of recycling in our county"

Answer: C. "What items do we recycle in our county?"
Remember that the difference between specificity and abstractness is a continuum. The most specific is something that is concrete and can be seen, heard, smelled, tasted, or felt, like cans, bottles, and newspapers. At the other end of the spectrum is an abstraction like importance. Lower-order questions are on the concrete end of the continuum; higher-order questions are on the abstract end.

30. **The teacher states that the lesson the students will be engaged in will consist of a review of the material from the previous day, a demonstration of the scientific principles of an electronic circuit, and small group work on setting up an electronic circuit. What has the teacher demonstrated?**

   A. The importance of reviewing
   B. Giving the general framework for the lesson to facilitate learning
   C. Giving students the opportunity to leave if they are not interested in the lesson
   D. Providing momentum for the lesson

Answer: B. Giving the general framework for the lesson to facilitate learning
If children know where they're going, they're more likely to be engaged in getting there. It's important to give them a road map whenever possible for what is coming in their classes.

31. **Wait-time has what effect?**

    A. Gives structure to the class discourse
    B. Fewer chain and low level questions are asked with more high-level questions included
    C. Gives the students time to evaluate the response
    D. Gives the opportunity for in-depth discussion about the topic

Answer: B. Fewer chain and low level questions are asked with more high-level questions included

One part of the questioning process for the successful teacher is *wait-time*: the time between the question and either the student response or your follow-up. Many teachers vaguely recommend some general amount of wait-time (until the student starts to get uncomfortable or is clearly perplexed), but we focus here on wait-time as a specific and powerful communicative tool that speaks through its structured silences. Embedded in wait-time are subtle clues about your judgments of a student's abilities and your expectations of individuals and groups. For example, the more time you allow a student to mull through a question, the more you trust his or her ability to answer that question without getting flustered. As a rule, the practice of prompting is not a problem. Giving support and helping students reason through difficult conundrums is part of being an effective teacher.

32. **What is one benefit of amplifying a student's response?**

   A. It helps the student develop a positive self-image
   B. It is helpful to other students who are in the process of learning the reasoning or steps in answering the question
   C. It allows the teacher to cover more content
   D. It helps to keep the information organized

Answer: B. It is helpful to other students who are in the process of learning the reasoning or steps in answering the question

Not only does the teacher show acceptance and give value to student responses by acknowledging, amplifying, discussing or restating the comment or question, she also helps the rest of the class learn to reason. If a student response is allowed, even if it is blurted out, it must be acknowledged and the student made aware of the quality of the response. A teacher acknowledges a student response by commenting on it. For example, the teacher states the definition of a noun, and then asks for examples of nouns in the classroom. A student responds, "My pencil is a noun." The teacher answers, "Okay, let us list that on the board." By this response and the action of writing "pencil" on the board, the teacher has just incorporated the student's response into the lesson. A teacher may also amplify the student response through another question directed to either the original student or to another student. For example, the teacher may say, "Okay," giving the student feedback on the quality of the answer, and then add, "What do you mean by "run" when you say the battery runs the radio?" Another way of showing acceptance and value of student response is to discuss the student response. For example, after a student responds, the teacher would say, "Class, let us think along that line. What is some evidence that proves what Susie just stated?" The teacher may also restate the response. For example, the teacher might say, "So you are saying the seasons are caused by the tilt of the Earth. Is this what you said?"

33. **A study by Darch and Gersten that examined the effects of positive feedback on the reading performance of seven and eight-year old learning disabled students found which result?**

   A. Students exhibited more self-esteem
   B. Students exhibited more on-task behavior
   C. Students were willing to answer more questions
   D. Students worked better in small groups

Answer: B. Students exhibited more on-task behavior

These two special educators have conducted many studies that are useful in dealing with "exceptional" children. Their findings are influencing the approaches to teaching special education students in many ways, but they are also useful for teachers in regular classrooms who have students who are struggling to keep up. The successful teacher will make use of their findings.

34. **When is optimal benefit reached when handling an incorrect student response?**

    A. When specific praise is used
    B. When the other students are allowed to correct that student
    C. When the student is redirected to a better problem solving approach
    D. When the teacher asks simple questions, provides cues to clarify, or gives assistance for working out the correct response

Answer: C. When the student is redirected to a better problem solving approach
It's important that students feel confident and comfortable in making responses, knowing that even if they give a wrong answer, they will not be embarrassed. If a student is ridiculed or embarrassed by an incorrect response, the student my shut down and not participate thereafter in classroom discussion. One way to respond to the incorrect answer is to ask the child, "Show me from your book why you think that." This gives the student a chance to correct the answer and redeem himself or herself. Another possible response from the teacher is to use the answer as a non-example. For example, after discussing the characteristics of warm-blooded and cold-blooded animals, the teacher asks for some examples of warm-blooded animals. A student raises his or her hand and responds, "A snake." The teacher could then say, "Remember, snakes lay eggs; they do not have live births. However, a snake is a good non-example of a mammal." The teacher then draws a line down the board and under a heading of "non-example" writes "snake." This action conveys to the child that even though the answer was wrong, it still contributed positively to the class discussion. Notice how the teacher did not digress from the task of listing warm-blooded animals, which in other words is maintaining academic focus, and at the same time allowed the student to maintain dignity.

35. **What are the two ways concepts can be taught?**

    A. Factually and interpretively
    B. Inductively and deductively
    C. Conceptually and inductively
    D. Analytically and facilitatively

Answer: B. Inductively and deductively
Induction is reasoning from the particular to the general—that is, looking at a feature that exists in several examples and drawing a conclusion about that feature. Deduction is the reverse: it's the statement of the generality and then supporting it with specific examples.

36. **Using pro-active expressions and repetition has what effect on students?**

    A. Helps student become aware of important elements of content
    B. Helps students develop positive self-esteem
    C. Helps students tolerate the lecture format of instruction
    D. Helps students to complete homework correctly

Answer: A. Helps student become aware of important elements of content
Refer to explanation for question 32.

37. **How can the teacher help students become more work oriented and less disruptive?**

    A. Seek their input for content instruction
    B. Challenge the students with a task and show genuine enthusiasm for it
    C. Use behavior modification techniques with all students
    D. Make sure lesson plans are complete for the week

Answer: B. Challenge the students with a task and show genuine enthusiasm for it
Many studies have demonstrated that the enthusiasm of the teacher is infectious. If students feel that the teacher is ambivalent about a task, they will also catch that attitude.

38. **What is an effective way to prepare students for testing?**

    A. Minimize the importance of the test
    B. Orient the students to the test, telling them of the purpose, how the results will be used and how it is relevant to them
    C. Use the same format for every test given
    D. Have them construct an outline to study from

Answer: B. Orient the students to the test, telling them of the purpose, how the results will be used and how it is relevant to them
If a test is to be an accurate measure of achievement, it must test the information, not the format of the test itself. If students know ahead of time what the test will be like, why they are taking it, what the teacher will do with the results, and what it has to do with them, the exercise is more likely to result in a true measure of what they've learned.

39. **How will students have a fair chance to demonstrate what they know on a test?**

   A. The examiner has strictly enforced rules for taking the test
   B. The examiner provides a comfortable setting free of distractions and positively encourages the students
   C. The examiner provides frequent stretch breaks to the students
   D. The examiner stresses the importance of the test to the overall grade

Answer: B. The examiner provides a comfortable setting free of distractions and positively encourages the students
Taking a test is intimidating to students at best. In addition, some students are unable to focus when there are distractions. Feeling that the teacher is on their side helps students relax and truly demonstrate what they have learned on a test.

40. **What is an example of formative feedback?**

   A. The results of an intelligence test
   B. Correcting the tests in small groups
   C. Verbal behavior that expresses approval of a student response to a test item
   D. Scheduling a discussion prior to the test

Answer: C. Verbal behavior that expresses approval of a student response to a test item
Standardized testing is currently under great scrutiny but educators agree that any test that serves as a means of gathering and interpreting information about children's learning and which can provide accurate, helpful input for nurturing children's further growth is acceptable. All testing must be formative in nature. Formative evaluation is the basic, everyday kind of assessment that teachers continually do to understand students' growth and to help them learn further.

41. How could a KWL chart be used in instruction?

    A. To motivate students to do a research paper
    B. To assess prior knowledge of the students
    C. To assist in teaching skills
    D. To put events in sequential order

Answer: B. To assess prior knowledge of the students
To understand information, not simply repeat it, students must connect it to their previous understanding. Textbooks can't do that. Instead, teachers—the people who know students best—have to find out what they know and how to build on that knowledge. In science, having students make predictions before conducting experiments is an obvious way of finding out what they know, and having them compare their observations to those predictions helps connect new knowledge and old. In history, teachers can also ask students what they know about a topic before they begin studying it or ask them to make predictions about what they will learn. KWL charts, in which students discuss what they know, what they want to know, and (later) what they have learned, are one way to activate this prior knowledge.

42. How can the teacher establish a positive climate in the classroom?

    A. Help students see the unique contributions of individual differences
    B. Use whole group instruction for all content areas
    C. Help students divide into cooperative groups based on ability
    D. Eliminate teaching strategies that allow students to make choices

Answer: A. Help students see the unique contributions of individual differences
In the first place, an important purpose of education is to prepare students to live successfully in the real world, and this is an important insight and understanding for them to take into that world. In the second place, the most fertile learning environment is one in which all viewpoints and backgrounds are respected and where everyone has equal respect.

43. How can students use a computer desktop publishing center?

   A. To set up a classroom budget
   B. To create student made books
   C. To design a research project
   D. To create a classroom behavior management system

Answer: B. To create student made books
By creating a book, students gain new insights into how communication works. Suddenly, the concept of audience for what they write and create becomes real. They also have an opportunity to be introduced to graphic arts, an exploding field. In addition, just as computers are a vital part of the world they will be entering as adults, so is desktop publishing. It is universally used by businesses of all kinds.

44. Which of the following is an example of a synthesis question according to Bloom's taxonomy?

   A. "What is the definition of_____?"
   B. "Compare _____ to _____."
   C. "Match column A to column B."
   D. "Propose an alternative to_____."

Answer: D. "Propose an alternative to_____."
There are six levels to the taxonomy: Knowledge, Comprehension, Application, Analysis, Synthesis, and Evaluation. Synthesis is compiling information together in a different way by combining elements in a new pattern or proposing alternative solutions to produce a unique communication, plan, or proposed set of operations or to derive a set of abstract relations.

45. What is a good strategy for teaching ethnically diverse students?

   A. Don't focus on the students' culture
   B. Expect them to assimilate easily into your classroom
   C. Imitate their speech patterns
   D. Include ethnic studies in the curriculum

Answer: D. Include ethnic studies in the curriculum
Exploring students' own cultures increases their confidence levels in the group. It is also a very useful tool when students are struggling to develop identities that they can feel comfortable with. The bonus is that this is good training for living in the world.

46. **How many stages of intellectual development does Piaget define?**

A. Two
B. Four
C. Six
D. Eight

Answer: B. Four
The stages are:

1. Sensorimotor stage: from birth to age 2 years (children experience the world through movement and senses)
2. Preoperational stage: from ages 2 to 7(acquisition of motor skills)
3. Concrete operational stage: from ages 7 to 11 (children begin to think logically about concrete events)
4. Formal operational stage: after age 11 (development of abstract reasoning)

47. **What is the most significant development emerging in children at age two?**

A. Immune system develops
B. Socialization occurs
C. Language develops
D. Perception develops

Answer: C. Language develops
Language begins to develop in an infant not long after birth. Chomsky claims that children teach themselves to speak using the people around them for resources. Several studies of the sounds infants make in their cribs seem to support this. The first stage of meaningful sounds is the uttering of a word that obviously has meaning for the child, for example, "bird" when the child sees one flying through the air. Does the development of real language begin when the noun is linked with a verb ("bird fly")? When language begins and how it develops has been debated for a long time. It's useful for a teacher to investigate those theories and studies.

48. **According to Piaget, when does the development of symbolic functioning and language take place?**

    A. Concrete operations stage
    B. Formal operations stage
    C. Sensorimotor stage
    D. Preoperational stage

Answer: D. Preoperational stage
Although there is no general theory of cognitive development, the most historically influential theory was developed by Jean Piaget, a Swiss psychologist (1896-1980). His theory provided many central concepts in the field of developmental psychology. His theory concerned the growth of intelligence, which for Piaget meant the ability to more accurately represent the world and perform logical operations on representations of concepts grounded in the world. His theory concerns the emergence and acquisition of schemata - schemes of how one perceives the world - in "developmental stages," times when children are acquiring new ways of mentally representing information.

His theory is considered "constructivist," meaning that, unlike nativist theories (which describe cognitive development as the unfolding of innate knowledge and abilities) or empiricist theories (which describe cognitive development as the gradual acquisition of knowledge through experience), asserts that we construct our cognitive abilities through self-motivated action in the world. For his development of the theory, Piaget was awarded the Erasmus Prize.

49. **What is the learning theorist's view of language acquisition?**

    A. Language is shaped by the reinforcement children receive from their caretakers
    B. Language is the result of innate biological mechanisms
    C. Language results spontaneously
    D. Language is developed through systematic instruction

Answer: A. Language is shaped by the reinforcement children receive from their caretakers
Chomsky, for instance, conducted studies on children that revealed that they actually teach themselves their own language by using the adults around them for reference. When a baby is playing with various sounds and happens to say "mama," the family goes bananas, so the baby keeps that sound! And so forth. Parents and others, of course, take their roles as language purveyors seriously, pointing out a bird and repeating it for the child until the child begins to echo a facsimile of that sound, which is *rewarded* by the adult doing the "teaching." Once children are in school, many of the same principles are in place. If the teacher rewards a usage, either printed or spoken, the child will be more likely to forge ahead and add more opportunities for reward.

50. Bobby, a nine year-old, has been caught stealing frequently in the classroom. What might be a factor contributing to this behavior?

    A. Need for the items stolen
    B. Serious emotional disturbance
    C. Desire to experiment
    D. A normal stage of development

Answer: B. Serious emotional disturbance

Lying, stealing, and fighting are atypical behaviors that most children may exhibit occasionally, but if a child lies, steals, or fights regularly or blatantly then these behaviors may be indicative of emotional distress. Emotional disturbances in childhood are not uncommon and take a variety of forms. Usually these problems show up in the form of uncharacteristic behaviors. Most of the time, children respond favorably to brief treatment programs of psychotherapy. At other times, disturbances may need more intensive therapy and are harder to resolve. All stressful behaviors need to be addressed, and any type of chronic, antisocial behavior needs to be examined as a possible symptom of deep-seated emotional upset.

51. What does the validity of a test refer to?

    A. Its consistency
    B. Its usefulness
    C. Its accuracy
    D. The degree of true scores it provides

Answer: B. Its usefulness

The *Joint technical standards for educational and psychological testing* (APA, AERA, NCME, 1985) states: "Validity is the most important consideration in test evaluation. The concept refers to the appropriateness, meaningfulness and usefulness of *the specific inferences made from test scores*. Test validation is the process of accumulating evidence to support such inferences. A variety of inferences may be made from scores produced by a given test, and there are many ways of accumulating evidence to support any particular inference. Validity, however, is a unitary concept. Although evidence may be accumulated in many ways, validity always refers to the degree to which that evidence supports the inferences that are made from test scores."

52. **What is the best definition for an achievement test?**

   A. It measures mechanical and practical abilities
   B. It measures broad areas of knowledge that are the result of cumulative learning experiences
   C. It measures the ability to learn to perform a task
   D. It measures performance related to specific, recently acquired information

Answer: B. It measures broad areas of knowledge that are the result of cumulative learning experiences
The ways that a teacher uses test data is a meaningful aspect of instruction and may increase the motivation level of the students especially when this information is available in the form of feedback to the students. This feedback should indicate to the students what they need to do in order to improve their achievement. Frequent testing and feedback is most often an effective way to increase achievement.

53. **Which of the following is an accurate description of ESL students?**

   A. Remedial students
   B. Exceptional education students
   C. Are not a homogeneous group
   D. Feel confident in communicating in English when with their peers

Answer: C. Are not a homogeneous group
Because ESL students are often grouped in classes that take a different approach to teaching English than those for native speakers, it's easy to assume that they all present with the same needs and characteristics. Nothing could be further from the truth, even in what they need when it comes to learning English. It's important that their backgrounds and personalities be observed just as with native speakers. It was very surprising several years ago when Vietnamese children began arriving in American schools with little training in English and went on to excel in their classes, often even beyond their American counterparts. In many schools, there were Vietnamese merit scholars in the graduating classes.

54. **What is an effective way to help a non-English speaking student succeed in class?**

    A. Refer the child to a specialist
    B. Maintain an encouraging, success-oriented atmosphere
    C. Help them assimilate by making them use English exclusively
    D. Help them cope with the content materials you presently use

Answer: B. Maintain an encouraging, success-oriented atmosphere
Anyone who is in an environment where his language is not the standard one feels embarrassed and inferior. The student who is in that situation expects to fail. Encouragement is even more important for these students. They need many opportunities to succeed.

55. **What should be considered when evaluating textbooks for content?**

    A. Type of print used
    B. Number of photos used
    C. Free of cultural stereotyping
    D. Outlines at the beginning of each chapter

Answer: C. Free of cultural stereotyping
While textbook writers and publishers have responded to the need to be culturally diverse in recent years, a few texts are still being offered that don't meet these standards. When teachers have an opportunity to be involved in choosing textbooks, they can be watchdogs for the community in keeping the curriculum free of matter that reinforces bigotry and discrimination.

56. **How can text be modified for low-level ESL students?**

    A. Add visuals and illustrations
    B. Let students write definitions
    C. Change text to a narrative form
    D. Have students write details out from the text

Answer: A. Add visuals and illustrations
No matter what name we put on it, a book is a book. If students can see the object, not only will they be able to compare their own word for it, a useful tool in learning a new language, but the object can serve as a mnemonic device. The teacher might use actual objects in a classroom to facilitate learning the new language.

57. **Which of the following is considered a study skill?**

   A. Using graphs, tables, and maps
   B. Using a desk-top publishing program
   C. Explaining important vocabulary words
   D. Asking for clarification

Answer: A. Using graphs, tables, and maps
In studying, it is certainly true that "a picture is worth a thousand words." Not only are these devices useful in making a point clear, they are excellent mnemonic devices for remembering facts.

58. **When using a kinesthetic approach, what would be an appropriate activity?**

   A. List
   B. Match
   C. Define
   D. Debate

Answer: B. Match
Brain lateralization theory emerged in the 1970s and demonstrated that the left hemisphere appeared to be associated with verbal and sequential abilities whereas the right hemisphere appeared to be associated with emotions and with spatial, holistic processing. Although those particular conclusions continue to be challenged, it is clear that people concentrate, process, and remember new and difficult information under very different conditions. For example, auditory and visual perceptual strengths, passivity, and self-oriented or authority-oriented motivation often correlate with high academic achievement, whereas tactual and kinesthetic strengths, a need for mobility, nonconformity, and peer motivation often correlate with school underachievement (Dunn & Dunn, 1992, 1993). Understanding how students perceive the task of learning new information differently is often helpful in tailoring the classroom experience for optimal success.

59. **Etienne is an ESL student. He has begun to engage in conversation which produces a connected narrative. What developmental stage for second language acquisition is he in?**

   A. Early production
   B. Speech emergence
   C. Preproduction
   D. Intermediate fluency

Answer: D. Intermediate fluency
Attaining total fluency usually takes several years although the younger the learner, the shorter the time it takes.

60. **What is a roadblock to second language learning?**

   A. Students are forced to speak
   B. Students speak only when ready
   C. Mistakes are considered a part of learning
   D. The focus is on oral communication

Answer: A. Students are forced to speak

It's embarrassing for anyone who is in a foreign-language environment to be forced to expose his inability to use that language before he is ready. Being flexible with these students until they're ready to try their wings will shorten the time it will take to approach fluency.

61. **What do cooperative learning methods all have in common?**

   A. Philosophy
   B. Cooperative task/cooperative reward structures
   C. Student roles and communication
   D. Teacher roles

Answer: B. Cooperative task/cooperative reward structures

Cooperative learning situations, as practiced in today's classrooms, grew out of searches conducted by several groups in the early 1970's. Cooperative learning situations can range from very formal applications such as STAD (Student Teams-Achievement Divisions) and CIRC (Cooperative Integrated Reading and Composition) to less formal groupings known variously as "group investigation," "learning together," and "discovery groups." Cooperative learning as a general term is now firmly recognized and established as a teaching and learning technique in American schools. Since cooperative learning techniques are so widely diffused in the schools, it is necessary to orient students in the skills by which cooperative learning groups can operate smoothly, and thereby enhance learning. Students who cannot interact constructively with other students will not be able to take advantage of the learning opportunities provided by the cooperative learning situations and will furthermore deprive their fellow students of the opportunity for cooperative learning.

62. **Who developed the theory of multiple intelligences?**

   A. Bruner
   B. Gardner
   C. Kagan
   D. Cooper

Answer: B. Gardner

Howard Gardner's most famous work is probably *Frames of Mind*, which details seven dimensions of intelligence (Visual/Spatial Intelligence, Musical Intelligence, Verbal Intelligence, Logical/Mathematical Intelligence, Interpersonal Intelligence, Intrapersonal Intelligence, and Bodily/Kinesthetic Intelligence). Gardner's claim that pencil and paper IQ tests do not capture the full range of human intelligences has garnered much praise within the field of education but has also met criticism, largely from psychometricians. Since the publication of *Frames of Mind*, Gardner has additionally identified the 8th dimension of intelligence: Naturalist Intelligence, and is still considering a possible ninth—Existentialist Intelligence.

63. **According to research, what can be a result of specific teacher actions on behavior?**

   A. Increase in student misconduct
   B. Increase in the number of referrals
   C. Decrease in student participation
   D. Decrease in student retentions

Answer: A. Increase in student misconduct

Unfortunately, at times misbehavior is the result of specific teacher actions. There is considerable research that indicates that some teacher behavior is upsetting to students and increases the occurrence of student misbehavior. Such teacher behavior may include any action that a child perceives as being unfair, punitive remarks about the child, his behavior or his work, or harsh responses to the child.

Teachers also need to be aware that much of what they say and do can be motivating and may have a positive effect on students' achievement. Studies have been conducted to determine the impact of teacher behavior on student performance. Surprisingly, a teacher's voice can really make an impression on students. Teachers' voices have several dimensions—volume, pitch, rate, etc. A recent study on the effects of speech rate indicates that, although both boys and girls prefer to listen at the rate of about 200 words per minute, boys tend to prefer slower rates overall than girls.

This same study indicates that a slower rate of speech directly affects processing ability and comprehension. Other speech factors such as communication of ideas, communication of emotion, distinctness/pronunciation, quality variation and phrasing, correlate with teaching criterion scores. These scores show that "good" teachers ("good" meaning teachers who positively impact and motivate students) use more variety in speech than do "less effective" teachers. A teacher's speech skills can be strong motivating elements. A teacher's body language has an even greater effect on student achievement and ability to set and focus on goals. Teacher smiles provide support and give feedback about the teacher's affective state. A deadpan expression can actually be a detriment to the student's progress. Teacher frowns are perceived by students to mean displeasure, disapproval, and even anger. Studies also show that teacher posture and movement are indicators of the teacher's enthusiasm and energy, which emphatically influence student learning, attitudes, motivation, and focus on goals. Teachers have a greater efficacy on student motivation than any person other than parents.

64. **What is the definition of proactive classroom management?**

   A. Management that is constantly changing
   B. Management that is downplayed
   C. Management that gives clear and explicit instructions and rewards compliance
   D. Management that is designed by the students

Answer: C. Management that gives clear and explicit instructions and rewards compliance
Classroom management plans should be in place when the school year begins. Developing a management plan takes a proactive approach—that is, decide what behaviors will be expected of the class as a whole, anticipate possible problems, and teach the behaviors early in the school year. Involving the students in the development of the classroom rules lets the students know the rationale for the rules, and allows them to assume responsibility in the rules because they had a part in developing them.

65. **What might be a result if the teacher is distracted by some unrelated event in the instruction?**

   A. Students will leave the class
   B. Students will understand the importance of class rules
   C. Students will stay on-task longer
   D. Students will lose the momentum of the lesson

Answer: D. Students will lose the momentum of the lesson
The teacher who can attend to a task situation and an extraneous situation simultaneously without becoming immersed in either one is said to have "with-it-ness." This ability is absolutely imperative for teacher effectiveness and success. It can be a difficult task to address deviant behavior while sustaining academic flow, but this is a skill that teachers need to develop early in their careers and one that will become second nature, intuitive, instinctive. Teacher with-it-ness is defined as "teacher behavior that indicates to the students that the teacher knows what she is doing" at all times and at the same time can continue instruction. With-it-ness has been found to positively affect both classroom behavior management and student task involvement. Teachers who have been specially trained in with-it-ness, report positive correlation between their with-it-ness and reading achievement as well as reductions in student misbehaviors and disruptions.

66. **Why is praise for compliance important in classroom management?**

    A. Students will continue deviant behavior
    B. Desirable conduct will be repeated
    C. It reflects simplicity and warmth
    D. Students will fulfill obligations

Answer: B. Desirable conduct will be repeated
The tried-and-true principle that behavior that is rewarded will be repeated is demonstrated here. If other students laugh at a child's misbehavior, he will repeat it. On the other hand, if the teach rewards the behaviors she wants to see repeated, it is likely to happen.

67. **What is an effective amount of "wait time"?**

    A. 1 second
    B. 5 seconds
    C. 15 seconds
    D. 10 seconds

Answer: B. 5 seconds
In formal training, most preservice teachers are taught the art of questioning. One part of the questioning process is *wait-time*: the time between the question and either the student response or your follow-up. Many teachers vaguely recommend some general amount of wait-time (until the student starts to get uncomfortable or is clearly perplexed), but we focus here on wait-time as a specific and powerful communicative tool that speaks through its structured silences. Embedded in wait-time are subtle clues about your judgments of a student's abilities and your expectations of individuals and groups. For example, the more time you allow a student to mull through a question, the more you trust his or her ability to answer that question without getting flustered.
As a rule, the practice of prompting is not a problem. Giving support and helping students reason through difficult conundrums is part of being an effective teacher.

68. **Mr. Perez has the pictures and maps ready for his lesson. The movie is set up to go, and he tested the operation of the machine before the class came in. What is this an example of?**

A. Controlled interruptions
B. Housekeeping
C. Punctuality
D. Management transition

Answer: B. Housekeeping
Housekeeping is when a "teacher routinizes activities such as passing papers out, moving to get books, writing on the board, etc., and has materials prepared, procedures worked out, and everything in order." Additionally, effective teachers have highly planned lessons with all materials in order prior to class. This is referred to as management of instructional material and defines it as "teacher preparation of materials that are to be used for a particular segment of instruction readily available." In other words, if a teacher is going to utilize a chart or a map in a lesson, the chart or map is already prepared and in place in the classroom before class begins. Furthermore, all materials are copied and in order ready to pass out as needed. This results in the efficient distribution of materials and leads to less off-task time. Therefore, effective teachers routinize daily housekeeping activities to minimize the amount of time spent on them. Additionally, they have all materials prepared prior to class and in order to facilitate speedy distribution.

69. **How are standardized tests useful in assessment?**

A. For teacher evaluation
B. For evaluation of the administration
C. For comparison from school to school
D. For comparison to the population on which the test was normed

Answer: D. For comparison to the population on which the test was normed
While the efficacy of the standardized tests that are being used nationally has come under attack recently, they are actually the only device for comparing where an individual student stands with a wide range of peers. They also provide a measure for a program or a school to evaluate how their own students are doing as compared to the populace at large. Even so, they should not be the only measure upon which decisions are made or evaluations drawn. There are many other instruments for measuring student achievement that the teacher needs to consult and take into account.

70. **Ms. Smith says, "Yes, exactly what do you mean by 'It was the author's intention to mislead you.'" What does this illustrate?**

   A. Digression
   B. Restates response
   C. Probes a response
   D. Amplifies a response

Answer: C. Probes a response
From ancient times notable teachers such as Socrates have employed oral-questioning to enhance their discourse, to stimulate thinking, and/or to stir emotion among their audiences. Educational researchers and practitioners virtually all agree that teachers' effective use of questioning promotes student learning. Effective teachers continually develop their questioning skills.

71. **What is perhaps the most controversial issue in developmental psychology?**

   A. Interactionism
   B. Nature vs. nurture
   C. Relevance of IQ scores
   D. Change vs. external events

Answer: B. Nature vs. nurture
Nature versus nature is a shorthand expression for debates about the relative importance of an individual's innate qualities (nature) versus personal experiences (nurture) in determining or causing individual differences in physical and behavioral traits. The phrase was first used by Francis Galton, possibly in reference to Shakespeare's Caliban - "A devil, a born devil, on whose nature Nurture can never stick" (from *The Tempest*). The controversy has heated up since the genetic code has been broken and it has become common knowledge that each person's DNA makes him or her unique.

72.   A child exhibits the following symptoms: a lack of emotional responsivity, indifference to physical contact, abnormal social play, and abnormal speech. What is the likely diagnosis for this child?

    A. Separation anxiety
    B. Mental retardation
    C. Autism
    D. Hypochondria

Answer: C. Autism
According to many psychologists who have been involved with treating autistic children, it seems that these children have built a wall between themselves and everyone else, including their families and even their parents. They do not make eye contact with others and do not even appear to hear the voices of those who speak to them. They cannot empathize with others and have no ability to appreciate humor. The prognosis for autistic children is painfully discouraging. Only about five percent of autistic children become socially well adjusted in adulthood. Another twenty percent make fair social adjustments. The remaining seventy-five percent are socially incapacitated and must be supervised for the duration of their lives. Treatment may include outpatient psychotherapy, drugs, or long-term treatment in a residential center, but neither the form of treatment nor even the lack of treatment seems to make a difference in the long run.

73.   What is not a way that teachers show acceptance and give value to a student response?

    A. Acknowledging
    B. Correcting
    C. Discussing
    D. Amplifying

Answer: B. Correcting
There are ways to treat every answer as worthwhile even if it happens to be wrong. The objective is to keep students involved in the dialogue. If their efforts to participate are "rewarded" with what seems to them to be a rebuke or that leads to embarrassment, they will be less willing to respond the next time.

74. What is teacher with-it-ness?

A. Having adequate knowledge of subject matter
B. A skill that must be mastered to attain certification
C. Understanding the current fads and trends that affect students
D. Attending to two tasks at once

Answer: D. Attending to two tasks at once

The teacher who knows his/her class well and is "with-it" will be cognizant of what is happening in every corner of the classroom between and among the children at all times. It should be relatively easy to identify problems that occur during the school day since the teacher observes the students as they interact with one another. Should the teacher be unaware of problems between students, misbehavior will surely occur. At this point in time the teacher will then tune in to the child who is misbehaving and hopefully, will soon be able to see what is happening to cause misbehaviors. As with anything else, the best way to solve behavior problems is to prevent them. The "with-it" teacher frequently knows when and why problems will occur and will act to eliminate potential provocation. The simplest means of preventing conflict between students who are having a problem with one another is to give them their own space and to separate them.

Teacher with-it-ness is defined as "teacher behavior that indicates to the students that the teacher knows what they are doing" at all times and at the same time can continue instruction. With-it-ness has been found to positively affect both classroom behavior management and student task involvement. Teachers who have been specially trained in with-it-ness, report positive correlation between their with-it-ness and reading achievement as well as reductions in student misbehaviors and disruptions. Teacher training in with-it-ness techniques includes:

a) implementing positive questioning techniques
b) using alerting cues
c) giving goal-directed prompts
d) using a soft voice when making reprimands
e) integrating alternative behavior desists
f) applying concurrent and specific praise

Research in regard to teacher with-it-ness indicate that teachers who are comfortable with the above techniques and are "with-it" increase instructional time by at least twenty minutes per day and decrease deviant behavior significantly. Further, with-it-ness techniques have been found to apply to boys as well as girls, to emotionally disturbed children as well as non-disturbed children, and to both younger and older grade children. They also apply to the entire class as well as to individual students.

75. **What should the teacher do when a student is tapping a pencil on the desk during a lecture?**

    A. Stop the lesson and correct the student as an example to other students

    B. Walk over to the student and quietly touch the pencil as a signal for the student to stop

    C. Announce to the class that everyone should remember to remain quiet during the lecture

    D. Ignore the student, hoping he or she will stop

Answer: B. Walk over to the student and quietly touch the pencil as a signal for the student to stop

An assertive discipline plan should be developed as soon as the teacher meets the students. The students can become involved in developing and discussing the needs for the rules. Rules should be limited to four to six basic classroom rules that are simple to remember and positively stated (For example, raise hand to speak, instead of, don't talk without permission).

1. Recognize and remove roadblocks to assertive discipline. Replace negative expectation with positives, and set reasonable limits for the children.

2. Practice an assertive response style. That is, clearly state teacher expectations and expect the students to comply with them.

3. Set limits. Take into consideration the students' behavioral needs, the teacher's expectations, and set limits for behavior. Decide what you will do when the rules are broken or complied with.

4. Follow through promptly with the consequences when students break the rules. However, the students should clearly know in advance what to expect when a rule is broken. Conversely, also follow through with the promised rewards for compliance and good behavior. This reinforces the concept that individuals choose their behavior and that there are consequences for their behavior.

5. Devise a system of positive consequences. Positive consequences do not have to always be food or treats. However, rewards should not be promised if it is not possible to deliver them. The result is a more positive classroom.

SAMPLE CONSTRUCTED RESPONSE #1

Use the following scenario to complete the exercise:

In an age of accountability for student learning, many educators assume that sticking to standards and ensuring that each standard is covered explicitly is the safest and most prudent thing to do. However, there are still many educators that believe that standards can be covered, perhaps in a non-linear fashion, by engaging students in academic and cross-curricular projects. Those who believe that project-based instruction is more valuable suggest that students will enjoy their learning more and will still learn many important academic standards in the process. Those who believe that standards-driven learning is more valuable might argue that it is unfair to students to not cover each and every area that they will be tested on. They might also suggest that teaching standards in a linear fashion will provide greater clarity for students.

Exercise
In a response written for an audience of teachers, use your knowledge of learners and the learning environment to analyze and discuss the issue of standards-driven and project-based teaching.

Sample Response

When analyzing state standards, it is important to realize that while standards may look like a bunch of unconnected skills, they really do build upon one another. When evaluating what to teach and how to teach it, it is important to ensure that what is being taught can be defended by the standards. However, students need to feel that what they are learning is important beyond passing tests. For that reason, developing lessons, units, and projects that take students' varied learning styles into account and draw upon real-world examples and issues will make learning more fun, and it will ensure that all students learn. However, such lessons, units, and projects should be based on standards so that students have interesting, enjoyable, and student-centered ways of learning the information they are required to know.

While many educators argue that standards-driven instruction is the only way to ensure that students are prepared for testing, doing so alone will provide little opportunity for students to learn in ways that are natural for them. On the other hand, while many educators are convinced that doing anything other than project-based instruction will be boring for students, not paying significant attention to standards will ensure that students are not prepared for the complex academic tasks they will be required to master. In my first year as a high school Language Arts teacher, I know that it is important to focus both on standards as well as engaging, meaningful projects.

Evaluation

The assignment asked the candidate to analyze two claims, both at odds with each other. One side, suggesting that standards-driven instruction is more appropriate, seemingly goes against the other side, project-based instruction. Yet the candidate wrote an essay that effectively found the best of both methods. The essay demonstrates a deep knowledge of student learning, as well as contemporary issues of curriculum and instruction. It demonstrated knowledge of student engagement and standards-based instruction. Although the essay did not ask for the candidate to demonstrate the best of both models, its strength lies in the fact that it does indeed show how both methods have some limitations as well as some strengths. Putting both together with a good curricular example was effective.

SAMPLE CONSTRUCTED RESPONSE #2

Use the following scenario to complete the exercise:

<u>LEARNING GOAL</u>: Students will learn and apply new information through the use of hands-on activities.

Exercise

In a written response for an audience of teachers, identify a grade/age level and subject area for which you are prepared to teach. Then use your knowledge of instruction and assessment to describe a "hands-on" activity or lesson that would help students to learn and apply new information.

Sample Response
For a second grade math lesson, I might teach students about fractions. While fractions are difficult to learn students will quickly understand the concept of fractions if using manipulatives and hands-on activities.

First, I would draw a picture of a pie on the overhead. I would then start to draw lines all over the place—one piece would be very large, a few pieces would be quite small, and the last few would be regular pieces of pie. Students would recognize that the pieces are a variety of different sizes. I would then ask them to help me cut the pie so that my five guests would have a similar-sized slice.

The next step would be to get the students into small groups. I would give them cut-outs of a pizza, and I would ask them to determine how many slices they would need to make sure everyone got one similarly-sized slice, and then cut the pizza.

The final step of this "hands-on" lesson would be to have the groups show me what one-half a pizza would be. On each pizza, they would count up their slices. This would go on and on until they understand that one-half or one-quarter could constitute a variety of numbers of slices depending how many slices were cut for each pizza.

This activity would help students learn the concept of fractions by giving them a practical, simple method of seeing fractions. They would understand that one pizza could have many different combinations of slices. Overall, this is a fun, practical, and useful way to teach the very difficult concept of fractions.

Evaluation
This essay demonstrates a very good knowledge of "hands-on" activities in the teaching of math. It clearly shows how various concepts of instruction can be tailored for different learning styles and different instructional standards. The candidate shows a good working knowledge of the Subarea by demonstrating the importance of carefully designing a lesson in order to meet students' learning needs. The lesson is very clear, and directions are provided step-by-step. No element of instruction is left out. Furthermore, the essay ends with a very good overview of how this lesson would meet students' learning needs, and it argues convincingly for using hands-on methods to teach this concept. Finally, the candidate chose a topic for which hands-on instruction would be very appropriate.

SAMPLE CONSTRUCTED RESPONSE #3

Use the following scenario to complete the exercise:

Scenario

Half-way through the school year, a week after semester report cards are sent home, you get an email from a student's parent complaining that you gave her son low grades for no good reason. She suggests that she has heard nothing but complaints about your teaching and that if you were a better teacher, her son would not have such low grades. She wants to (a) meet with you and the principal together, (b) examine other students' grades to see how her son's grades compare, and (c) have you put together extra credit work so that her son can raise her grade.

Exercise

In a written response to an audience of educators, use your knowledge of the professional environment to:

- Identify the important issues at stake in this scenario.
- Describe a plan of action you would take to remedy this problem.
- Explain why your plan would be effective in resolving the issue.

Sample Response

The primary concern in this scenario is the difference of opinion about the student's academic standing in the class. This is an issue of assessment, but it is also an issue of politics, parent-school relations, and legalities.

First, I would inform the principal that a concern has come up regarding a student's grade. I would let the principal know my plan for dealing with this, and I would suggest that a meeting may be necessary. Even though I would have to come back to the principal to discuss the issue in further detail later, I would simply want the principal to know that an incident has occurred so that he/she would be informed and so that I could document that I have gone through all the proper chains of command.

Second, I would investigate my own grading practices, as well as the student's work. Because I would have documented progress and all grades carefully, as well as compiled portfolios of all my students' work, I would not have any problem in accessing the information I would need to determine if I had made an error in evaluation.

Third, I would convene a meeting with the student's parent and the principal. I would want to start by listening to the parent's concerns over her perceptions of my teaching. I would take those concerns seriously and write each one down to demonstrate respect. I would then review all the material I brought. However, I would want to end the meeting by offering a "win-win" solution. I would encourage the parent to work with me to determine how her son could get good grades for the next semester.

Of course, if I found an error in my evaluation, I would ensure that the grade be changed. However, under no circumstances would it be fair to offer extra credit to one student and not the others.

What this scenario tells me is that I would want to keep in constant contact with parents, particularly of students whose grades were low throughout the semester. As a summary, my method of dealing with this scenario shows respect in the student and parent, yet it relies on careful methods of evaluation of student progress.

Evaluation

This response offers a very detailed and comprehensive explanation of a strategy that could be followed for any disagreement about grades. What is most promising about this response is that it goes beyond the incident itself to show how respect, documentation, and full disclosure are important in the field of teaching. In many ways, it also demonstrates a careful process of applying fairness to the classroom.

SAMPLE EXTENDED ESSAY RESPONSE

Goal: Understand various instructional approaches and use this knowledge to facilitate student learning.

Examples of Teaching Objectives

Analyzing the uses, benefits, or limitations of a specific instructional approach (e.g., direct instruction, cooperative learning, interdisciplinary instruction, exploration, discovery learning, independent study, lectures, hands-on activities, peer tutoring, technology-based approach, various discussion methods such as guided discussion, various questioning methods) in relation to given purposes and learners.

Recognizing appropriate strategies for varying the role of the teacher (e.g., working with students as instructor, facilitator, observer; working with other adults in the classroom) in relation to the situation and the instructional approach used.

Comparing instructional approaches in terms of teacher and student responsibilities, expected student outcomes, usefulness for achieving instructional purposes, etc.

Exercise

In an essay written for a group of educators, frame your response by identifying a grade level and/or subject area for which you are prepared to teach; then:

- Explain the importance of using a variety of instructional approaches so that all students can learn and master the standards.
- Describe two strategies to meet this goal.
- Explain why the strategies you have chosen would be effective.

Be sure to specify a grade level/subject area in your essay, and frame your ideas so that an educator at your level will be able to understand the basis for your response.

Sample Response

It is importance to tailor instruction of difficult concepts to meet the needs of all students. To describe the importance of utilizing various instructional strategies and then to provide examples of useful strategies, I will illustrate with a hypothetical eighth grade Language Arts class.

First, since we know that all students have different styles of learning, by utilizing a wide range of strategies to teach the same concept, teachers ensure that as many learning styles as possible are satisfied. Let's consider a visual learner in a Language Arts classroom who only receives instruction orally. The teacher focuses on texts abstractly, and often discussion is utilized. The teacher rarely uses the board, never uses PowerPoint, and never allows students to demonstrate learning in artistic ways. While this visual learner may have the potential to achieve at a higher level, this may not occur as the instruction has missed his or her learning style entirely.

A second reason for varying instructional strategies is based on the concept of constructivism. Constructivism suggests that people develop concepts in their minds in highly personalized ways. Take a concept that might be taught in a ninth grade Language Arts class: hyperbole, a literary term for exaggeration. Effective strategies for teaching this concept include lecturing, pointing out examples in a text, and allowing students to develop their own examples of hyperbole. A combination of strategies enables students to have a more complete mental construct of the concepts.

A third reason for varying instructional strategies is based on student engagement. While eighth grade English teachers may enjoy talking about hyperbole, their students may not be so fascinated. By varying instructional strategies, students get opportunities to learn actively and in many different modalities. They experience concepts in different ways and involve themselves in various contexts of the concepts.

To illustrate how instructional strategies can be varied, I will briefly describe two unique strategies that a teacher might use to promote student learning of the concepts involved in developing and writing a research report.

The first strategy in this unit on research report writing comes at an early stage. As students are settling on topics and looking into books they might use to inform their reports, a teacher might have students conduct a first-hand investigation on their own. For example, a student interested in writing a report on an historical figure might interview a history teacher at the school. Or a student interested in writing about air pollution might conduct a small science experiment by testing the air quality on the side of a highway. The act of having students go out into the "field" helps them learn about the ways in which knowledge is generated. This strategy also promotes active, hands-on learning, and makes the experience more real for them, allowing them to become more engaged in the process.

A second strategy in this unit comes at the end of the process, as students' rough drafts are written. Students will review their drafts in small groups. Each student would have to read his or her paper aloud to the other students in the group while the group members listen and record comments. Then, each group member will comment on the paper for two to three minutes. After one student's paper is complete, then the group rotates to the next group member. This strategy is beneficial for many reasons. While many classrooms utilize peer review for student writing, by having students read their papers aloud, students experience a performance-type setting to the process, which is more engaging. Also, when students review peers' papers, they often focus on grammar and spelling, rather than more important aspects of clarity, content, and focus.

Utilizing various instructional strategies provides students with richer opportunities to learn concepts. It allows simplistic standards to come alive, and it promotes deeper learning. In general, teachers who use various instructional strategies will have livelier, learning-centered classrooms.

Evaluation
This paper would earn a high score for a variety of reasons. First, most importantly, it answers all parts of the question. It provides a framing grade level and subject. It focuses on a general conception of why utilizing various instructional strategies is beneficial for students. It provides two rich and well explained strategies as examples. And finally, it explains why those strategies would be effective for student learning. The examples focus on multiple areas of importance in instruction: student engagement, multiple learning styles, conceptual understanding, and student achievement.

TExES
GENERALIST
EC-6 191

READING, LANGUAGE, AND LITERATURE

1. While standing in line at the grocery store, three-year-old Megan says to her mother in a regular tone of voice, "Mom, why is that woman so fat?" What does this indicate a lack of understanding of?
    (Average)

    A. Syntax
    B. Semantics
    C. Morphology
    D. Pragmatics

2. Oral language development can be enhanced by which of the following?
    (Easy)

    A. Meaningful conversation
    B. Storytelling
    C. Alphabet songs
    D. All of the above

3. Ms. Chomski is presenting a new story to her class of first graders. In the story, a family visits their grandparents, where they all gather around a record player and listen to music. Many students do not understand what a record player is, especially some children for whom English is not their first language. Which of the following would be best for Ms. Chomski to do?
    (Rigorous)

    A. Discuss what a record player is with her students
    B. Compare a record player with a CD player
    C. Have students look up *record player* in a dictionary
    D. Show the students a picture of a record player

4. Reading aloud correlates with all of the following EXCEPT:
    (Rigorous)

    A. Reader self-confidence
    B. Better reading comprehension
    C. Literacy development
    D. Overall school success

5. **Mr. Johns is using an activity that involves having students analyze the public speaking of others. All of the following would be guidelines for this activity EXCEPT:**
(Rigorous)

A. The speeches to be evaluated are not given by other students
B. The rubric for evaluating the speeches includes pace, pronunciation, body language, word choice, and visual aids
C. The speeches to be evaluated are best presented live to give students a more engaging learning experience
D. One of Mr. Johns' goals with this activity is to help students improve their own public speaking skills

6. **All of the following are true about phonological awareness EXCEPT:**
(Average)

A. It may involve print
B. It is a prerequisite for spelling and phonics
C. Activities can be done by the children with their eyes closed
D. It starts before letter recognition is taught

7. **Which of the following explains a significant difference between phonics and phonemic awareness?**
(Rigorous)

A. Phonics involves print, while phonemic awareness involves language
B. Phonics is harder than phonemic awareness
C. Phonics involves sounds, while phonemic awareness involves letters
D. Phonics is the application of sounds to print, while phonemic awareness is oral

8. **Theorist Marilyn Jager Adams, who researches early reading, has outlined five basic types of phonemic awareness tasks. Which of the following is NOT one of the tasks noted by Jager Adams?**
(Average)

A. Ability to do oddity tasks
B. Ability to orally blend words and split syllables
C. Ability to sound out words when reading aloud
D. Ability to do phonics manipulation tasks

9. **Activities that parents can practice at home to improve phonological and phonemic awareness include which of the following?**
(Average)

   A. Play games with words that sound alike as you experience them in everyday home activities

   B. Demonstrate how sounds blend together in familiar words

   C. Play a game in which the goal is to find objects with names that begin with a certain initial sound

   D. All of the above

10. **The alphabetic principle can best be described by which of the following statements?**
(Rigorous)

   A. Most reading skills need to be acquired through a regular teaching of the alphabet

   B. Written words are composed of patterns of letters that represent the sounds of spoken words

   C. Written words are composed of patterns that must be memorized in order to read well

   D. Spoken words (regular and irregular) lead to phonological reading

11. **Which of the following is NOT true about multisensory approaches to teaching the alphabetic principle?**
(Rigorous)

   A. Some children can only learn through multisensory techniques

   B. Multisensory techniques give multiple cues to enhance memory and learning

   C. Quilt book, rhyme time, letter path, and shape game are multisensory strategies

   D. Multisensory techniques require direct teaching and ongoing engagement

12. **Activities that facilitate learning the alphabetic principle include:**
(Average)

   A. Read alouds, alphabet art, concept books, and name sorts

   B. Read alouds, shared reading, concept books, and picture books

   C. Picture books, concept books, and alphabet books

   D. Alphabet art, name sorts, shared reading, and phonics

13. **Which of the following is a convention of print that children learn during reading activities?**
(Rigorous)

A. The meaning of words
B. The left-to-right motion
C. The purpose of print
D. The identification of letters

14. **Alphabet books are classified as:**
(Average)

A. Concept books
B. Easy-to-read books
C. Board books
D. Picture books

15. **To determine an author's purpose, a reader must:**
(Rigorous)

A. Use his or her own judgment
B. Verify all the facts
C. Link the causes to the effects
D. Rely on common sense

16. **To decode is to:**
(Easy)

A. Construct meaning
B. Sound out a printed sequence of letters
C. Use a special code to decipher a message
D. None of the above

17. **Contextual redefinition is a strategy that encourages children to use the context more effectively by presenting them with sufficient vocabulary _____ the reading of a text.**
(Rigorous)

A. after
B. before
C. during
D. none of the above

18. **What is the best place for students to find appropriate synonyms, antonyms, and other related words to enhance their writing?**
(Average)

A. Dictionary
B. Spell check
C. Encyclopedia
D. Thesaurus

19. **Which of the following indicates that a student is a fluent reader?**
(Easy)

A. Reads texts with expression or prosody
B. Reads word to word and haltingly
C. Must intentionally decode a majority of the words
D. In a writing assignment, sentences are poorly organized structurally

20. **Which of the following reading strategies is NOT associated with fluent reading abilities?**
(Average)

A. Pronouncing unfamiliar words by finding similarities with familiar words
B. Establishing a purpose for reading
C. Formulating questions about the text while reading
D. Reading sentences word by word

21. **Automaticity refers to all of the following EXCEPT:**
(Rigorous)

A. Automatic whole-word identification
B. Automatic recognition of syllable types
C. Automatic reactions to the content of a paragraph
D. Automatic identification of graphemes as they relate to four basic word types

22. **Which of the following activities are likely to improve fluency?**
(Easy)

A. Partner reading and a reading theater
B. Phrased reading
C. Both A and B
D. None of the above

23. **Students are about to read a text that contains words that will need to be understood for the students to understand the text. When should the vocabulary be introduced to students?**
(Average)

A. Before reading
B. During reading
C. After reading
D. It should not be introduced

24. **Which of the following is an important feature of vocabulary instruction, according to the National Reading Panel?**
(Average)

A. Repetition of vocabulary items
B. Keeping a consistent task structure at all times
C. Teaching vocabulary in more than one language
D. Isolating vocabulary instruction from other subjects

25. **A sixth-grade science teacher has given her class a paper to read on the relationship between food and weight gain. The writing contains signal words and phrases such as "because," "consequently," "this is how," and "due to." This paper has which text structure?**
(Rigorous)

A. Cause and effect
B. Compare and contrast
C. Description
D. Sequencing

26. **Which of the following is not a strategy of teaching reading comprehension?**
(Rigorous)

A. Asking questions
B. Utilizing graphic organizers
C. Focusing on mental images
D. Manipulating sounds

27. **The children's literature genre came into its own in the:**
(Easy)

A. Seventeenth century
B. Eighteenth century
C. Nineteenth century
D. Twentieth century

28. **When evaluating reference sources, students should do all of the following EXCEPT:**
(Rigorous)

A. Look for self-published books by the author as evidence of expert status
B. Examine the level of detail provided by the source
C. Review the references at the end of the book or article
D. See if the author presents both sides of an argument or viewpoint

29. **Graphic organizers:**
(Average)

A. are used primarily in grades K-3
B. work better with poetry than other forms of writing
C. help readers think critically by pulling out the main idea and supporting details
D. generally aren't helpful to ELL students

30. **Which of the following helps students in a way that is similar to using a glossary?**
(Average)

A. Information in the text such as charts, graphs, maps, diagrams, captions, and photos
B. Prewriting
C. Classroom discussion of the main idea
D. Paired reading

31. **Which of these describes the best way to teach spelling?**
(Rigorous)

A. At the same time that grammar and sentence structure are taught
B. Within the context of meaningful language experiences
C. Independently so that students can concentrate on spelling
D. In short lessons, as students pick up spelling almost immediately

32. **Which of the following sentences contains an error in agreement?**
(Rigorous)

A. Jennifer is one of the women who writes for the magazine.
B. Each one of their sons plays a different sport.
C. This band has performed at the Odeum many times.
D. The data are available online at the listed Web site.

33. **All of the following are correctly punctuated EXCEPT:**
(Rigorous)

A. "The airplane crashed on the runway during takeoff."
B. I was embarrassed when Ms. White said, "Your slip is showing!"
C. "The middle school readers were unprepared to understand Bryant's poem 'Thanatopsis.'"
D. The hall monitor yelled, "Fire! Fire!"

34. **Which of the following is not a technique of prewriting?**
(Average)

A. Clustering
B. Listing
C. Brainstorming
D. Proofreading

35. **Which of the following is NOT a prewriting strategy?**
(Average)

A. Analyzing sentences for variety
B. Keeping an idea book
C. Writing in a daily journal
D. Writing down whatever comes to mind

36. A student has written a paper with the following characteristics: written in first person; characters, setting, and plot; some dialogue; events organized in chronological sequence with some flashbacks. In what genre has the student written?
(Easy)

A. Expository writing
B. Narrative writing
C. Persuasive writing
D. Technical writing

37. Exposition occurs within a story:
(Rigorous)

A. After the rising action
B. After the denouement
C. Before the rising action
D. Before the setting

38. Which of the following messages provides the most accessibility to the most learners?
(Average)

A. Print message
B. Audiovisual message
C. Graphic message
D. Audio message

39. Which of the following advertising techniques is based on appealing to our desire to think for ourselves?
(Easy)

A. Celebrity endorsement
B. Intelligence
C. Independence
D. Lifestyle

40. Which of the following is NOT useful in creating visual media for the classroom?
(Average)

A. Limit your graph to just one idea or concept and keep the content simple
B. Balance substance and visual appeal
C. Match the information to the format that will fit it best
D. Make sure to cite all references to copyrighted material

41. All of the following are examples of ongoing informal assessment techniques used to observe student progress EXCEPT:
(Rigorous)

A. Analysis of student work product
B. Collection of data from assessment tests
C. Effective questioning
D. Observation of students

42. **Which of the following is a formal reading-level assessment?**
(Easy)

A. A standardized reading test
B. A teacher-made reading test
C. An interview
D. A reading diary

43. **Which of the following is NOT considered a reading level?**
(Easy)

A. Independent
B. Instructional
C. Intentional
D. Frustrational

44. **Which of the following are good choices for supporting a thesis?**
(Rigorous)

A. Reasons
B. Examples
C. Answer to the question, "why?"
D. All of the above

45. **Which of the following should not be included in the opening paragraph of an informative essay?**
(Rigorous)

A. Thesis sentence
B. Details and examples supporting the main idea
C. A broad general introduction to the topic
D. A style and tone that grabs the reader's attention

MATHEMATICS

46. **Which of the following is a true statement regarding manipulatives in mathematics instruction?**
(Average)

A. Manipulatives are materials that students can physically handle
B. Manipulatives help students make concrete concepts abstract
C. Manipulatives include fingers, tiles, paper folding, and ice cream sticks
D. Manipulatives help students make abstract concepts concrete

47. **All of the following are tools that can strengthen students' mathematical understanding EXCEPT:**
(Easy)

A. Rulers, scales, and protractors
B. Calculators, counters, and measuring containers
C. Software and hardware
D. Money and software

48. **Which of the following is not a good example of helping students make connections between the real world and mathematics?**
(Average)

A. Studying a presidential election from the perspective of the math involved
B. Using weather concepts to teach math
C. Having student helpers take attendance
D. Reviewing major mathematical theorems on a regular basis

49. **Which of the following is an example of the associative property?**
(Rigorous)

A. $a(b + c) = ab + bc$
B. $a + 0 = a$
C. $(a + b) + c = a + (b + c)$
D. $a + b = b + a$

50. **What is the greatest common factor of 16, 28, and 36?**
(Easy)

A. 2
B. 4
C. 8
D. 16

51. **Mathematical operations are done in the following order:**
(Rigorous)

A. Simplify inside grouping characters such as parentheses, brackets, square roots, fraction bars, etc.; multiply out expressions with exponents; do multiplication or division, from left to right; do addition or subtraction, from left to right
B. Do multiplication or division, from left to right; simplify inside grouping characters such as parentheses, brackets, square roots, fraction bars, etc.; multiply out expressions with exponents; do addition or subtraction, from left to right
C. Simplify inside grouping characters such as parentheses, brackets, square roots, fraction bars, etc.; do addition or subtraction, from left to right; multiply out expressions with exponents; do multiplication or division, from left to right
D. None of the above

52. **Which of the following is an irrational number?**
(Rigorous)

A. .36262626262…
B. 4
C. 8.2
D. -5

53. **The number "0" is a member of all of the following groups of numbers EXCEPT:**
(Rigorous)

A. Whole numbers
B. Real numbers
C. Natural numbers
D. Integers

54. **4,087,361: What number represents the ten thousands' place?**
(Easy)

A. 4
B. 6
C. 0
D. 8

55. **Two mathematics classes have a total of 410 students. The 8:00 a.m. class has 40 more students than the 10:00 a.m. class. How many students are in the 10:00 a.m. class?**
(Average)

A. 123.3
B. 370
C. 185
D. 330

56. **Three-dimensional figures in geometry are called:**
(Easy)

A. Solids
B. Cubes
C. Polygons
D. Blocks

57. **The volume is:**
(Easy)

A. Area of the faces excluding the bases
B. Total area of all the faces, including the bases
C. The number of cubic units in a solid
D. The measure around the object

58. **If a right triangle has legs with the measurements of 3 cm and 4 cm, what is the measure of the hypotenuse?**
(Average)

A. 6 cm
B. 1 cm
C. 7 cm
D. 5 cm

59. **If the radius of a right circular cylinder is doubled, how does its volume change?**
(Rigorous)

A. No change
B. Also is doubled
C. Four times the original
D. Pi times the original

60. **Find the area of a rectangle if you know that the base is 8 cm and the diagonal of the rectangle is 8.5 cm:** *(Rigorous)*

A. 24 cm²
B. 30 cm²
C. 18.9 cm²
D. 24 cm

61. **An item that sells for $375.00 is put on sale at $120.00. What is the percentage of decrease?** *(Average)*

A. 25%
B. 28%
C. 68%
D. 34%

62. **What is a translation?** *(Rigorous)*

A. To turn a figure around a fixed point
B. When the object has the same shape and same size, but figures face in different directions
C. To "slide" an object a fixed distance in a given direction
D. The transformation that "shrinks" or "makes it bigger"

63. **What measures could be used to report the distance traveled in walking around a track?** *(Easy)*

A. Degrees
B. Square meters
C. Kilometers
D. Cubic feet

64. **Corporate salaries are listed for several employees. Which would be the best measure of central tendency?** *(Average)*

$24,000	$24,000
$26,000	$28,000
$30,000	$120,000

A. Mean
B. Median
C. Mode
D. No difference

65. **Given a drawer with 5 black socks, 3 blue socks, and 2 red socks, what is the probability that you will draw two black socks in two draws in a dark room?** *(Rigorous)*

A. 2/9
B. 1/4
C. 17/18
D. 1/18

66. **Suppose you have a bag of marbles that contains 2 red marbles, 5 blue marbles, and 3 green marbles. If you replace the first marble chosen, what is the probability you will choose 2 green marbles in a row?**
(Average)

A. 2/5
B. 9/100
C. 9/10
D. 3/5

67. **In probability, the sample space represents:**
(Average)

A. An outcome of an experiment
B. A list of all possible outcomes of an experiment
C. The number of times you must flip a coin
D. The amount of room needed to conduct an experiment

68. **Deduction is:**
(Average)

A. Logical reasoning
B. The process of arriving at a conclusion based on other statements that   are known to be true
C. Both A and B
D. Neither A nor B

69. **Find the inverse of the following statement: If I like dogs, then I do not like cats.**
(Rigorous)

A. If I like dogs, then I do like cats.
B. If I like cats, then I like dogs.
C. If I like cats, then I do not like dogs.
D. If I do not like dogs, then I like cats.

70. **Find the converse of the following statement: If I like math, then I do not like science.**
(Average)

A. If I do not like science, then I like math.
B. If I like math, then I do not like science.
C. If I do not like math, then I do not like science.
D. If I like math, then I do not like science.

71. **Which of the following is the basic language of mathematics?**
(Easy)

A. Symbolic representation
B. Number lines
C. Arithmetic operations
D. Deductive thinking

72. **The mass of a cookie is closest to:**
(Easy)

A. 0.5 kg
B. 0.5 grams
C. 15 grams
D. 1.5 grams

HISTORY AND SOCIAL SCIENCE

73. **Using graphics can enhance the presentation of social science information because:**
(Average)

A. They can explain complex relationships among various data points
B. Charts and graphs summarize information well
C. Maps can describe geographic distribution of historical information
D. All of the above

74. **All of the following are key elements in planning a child-centered curriculum EXCEPT:**
(Rigorous)

A. Referring students who need special tutoring
B. Identifying students' prior knowledge and skills
C. Sequencing learning activities
D. Specifying behavioral objectives

75. **The Texas Assessment of Knowledge and Skills (TAKS) test is an example of:**
(Average)

A. Criterion-referenced assessment
B. Norm-referenced assessment
C. Performance-based assessment
D. Other type of assessment

76. **Ms. Gomez has a number of ESOL students in her class. In order to meet their specific needs as second-language learners, which of the following would NOT be an appropriate approach?**
(Easy)

A. Pair students of different ability levels for English practice
B. Focus most of her instruction on teaching English rather than content
C. Provide accommodations during testing and with assignments
D. Use visual aids to help students make word links with familiar objects

77. **Which one of the following is NOT a reason why Europeans came to the New World?**
(Rigorous)

A. To find resources in order to increase wealth
B. To establish trade
C. To increase a ruler's power and importance
D. To spread Christianity

78. **Which of the following were results of the Age of Exploration?**
(Easy)

A. More complete and accurate maps and charts
B. New and more accurate navigational instruments
C. Proof that the Earth is round
D. All of the above

79. **The belief that the United States should control all of North America was called:**
(Easy)

A. Westward expansion
B. Pan Americanism
C. Manifest Destiny
D. Nationalism

80. **Nationalism can be defined as the division of land and resources according to which of the following?**
(Rigorous)

  A. Religion, race, or political ideology
  B. Religion, race, or gender
  C. Historical boundaries, religion, or race
  D. Race, gender, or political ideology

81. **The study of the social behavior of minority groups would be in the area of:**
(Average)

  A. Anthropology
  B. Psychology
  C. Sociology
  D. Cultural geography

82. **"Participant observation" is a method of study most closely associated with and used in:**
(Rigorous)

  A. Anthropology
  B. Archaeology
  C. Sociology
  D. Political science

83. **For the historian studying ancient Egypt, which of the following would be least useful?**
(Rigorous)

  A. The record of an ancient Greek historian on Greek-Egyptian interaction
  B. Letters from an Egyptian ruler to his/her regional governors
  C. Inscriptions on stele of the fourteenth Egyptian dynasty
  D. Letters from a nineteenth-century Egyptologist to his wife

84. **The term *sectionalism* refers to:**
(Easy)

  A. Different regions of the continent
  B. Issues between the North and South
  C. Different regions of the country
  D. Different groups of countries

85. **Which political group pushed the Reconstruction measures through Congress after Lincoln's death?**
(Rigorous)

  A. The Radical Republicans
  B. The Radical Democrats
  C. The Whigs
  D. The Independents

86. **As a result of the Missouri Compromise:**
(Average)

A. Slavery was not allowed in the Louisiana Purchase
B. The Louisiana Purchase was nullified
C. Louisiana separated from the Union
D. The Embargo Act was repealed

87. **Which country was a cold war foe of the United States?**
(Easy)

A. Soviet Union
B. Brazil
C. Canada
D. Argentina

88. **The international organization established to work for world peace at the end of the Second World War was the:**
(Average)

A. League of Nations
B. United Federation of Nations
C. United Nations
D. United World League

89. **What event triggered World War I?**
(Average)

A. The fall of the Weimar Republic
B. The resignation of the czar
C. The assassination of Austrian Archduke Ferdinand
D. The assassination of the czar

90. **What is the most significant environmental change in Texas over the last century?**
(Rigorous)

A. The number of square miles devoted to living space
B. Continued exploration for oil and gas
C. Development along the Gulf Coast
D. Changes in agricultural practices

91. **The end to hunting, gathering, and fishing of prehistoric people was due to:**
(Average)

A. Domestication of animals
B. Building crude huts and houses
C. Development of agriculture
D. Organized government in villages

92. **Which of the following is most useful in showing differences in variables at a specific point in time?**
(Average)

   A. Histogram
   B. Scatter plots
   C. Pie chart
   D. Bar graph

93. **Capitalism and communism are alike in that they are both:**
(Easy)

   A. Organic systems
   B. Political systems
   C. Centrally planned systems
   D. Economic systems

94. **During the 1920s, the United States almost completely stopped all immigration. One of the reasons was:**
(Rigorous)

   A. Plentiful, cheap unskilled labor was no longer needed by industrialists
   B. War debts from World War I made it difficult to render financial assistance
   C. European nations were reluctant to allow people to leave since there was a need to rebuild populations and economic stability
   D. The United States did not become a member of the League of Nations

95. **In the 1800s, the era of industrialization and growth was characterized by:**
(Average)

   A. Small firms
   B. Public ownership
   C. Worker-owned enterprises
   D. Monopolies and trusts

96. **Which one of the following would NOT be considered a result of World War II?**
(Rigorous)

   A. Economic depressions and slow resumption of trade and financial aid
   B. Western Europe was no longer the center of world power
   C. The beginnings of new power struggles, not only in Europe but in Asia as well
   D. Territorial and boundary changes for many nations, especially in Europe

97. **The New Deal was:**
(Average)

   A. A trade deal with England
   B. A series of programs to provide relief during the Great Depression
   C. A new exchange rate regime
   D. A plan for tax relief

98. **Which of the following is an example of a direct democracy?**
(Average)

A. Elected representatives
B. Greek city-states
C. The Constitution
D. The Confederate states

99. **Many governments in Europe today have which of the following type of government?**
(Average)

A. Absolute monarchies
B. Constitutional governments
C. Constitutional monarchies
D. Another form of government

SCIENCE

100. **Accepted procedures for preparing solutions include the use of:**
(Easy)

A. Alcohol
B. Hydrochloric acid
C. Distilled water
D. Tap water

101. **Laboratory activities contribute to student performance in all of the following domains EXCEPT:**
(Average)

A. Process skills such as observing and measuring
B. Memorization skills
C. Analytical skills
D. Communication skills

102. **Which is the correct order of methodology?**
(Average)

1. Collecting data.
2. Planning a controlled experiment.
3. Drawing a conclusion.
4. Hypothesizing a result.
5. Revisiting a hypothesis to answer a question.

A. 1, 2, 3, 4, 5
B. 4, 2, 1, 3, 5
C. 4, 5, 1, 3, 2
D. 1, 3, 4, 5, 2

103. **In an experiment measuring the growth of bacteria at different temperatures, what is the independent variable?**
(Rigorous)

A. Number of bacteria
B. Growth rate of bacteria
C. Temperature
D. Size of bacteria

104. **Which of the following is a misconception about the task of teaching science in elementary school?**
(Average)

A. Teach facts as a priority over teaching how to solve problems.
B. Involve as many senses as possible in the learning experience.
C. Accommodate individual differences in pupils' learning styles.
D. Consider the effect of technology on people rather than on material things.

105. **Which of the following is the most accurate definition of a nonrenewable resource?**
(Rigorous)

A. A nonrenewable resource is never replaced once used
B. A nonrenewable resource is replaced on a time scale that is very long relative to human life spans
C. A nonrenewable resource is a resource that can only be manufactured by humans
D. A nonrenewable resource is a species that has already become extinct

106. **All of the following are hormones in the human body EXCEPT:**
(Average)

A. Cortisol
B. Testosterone
C. Norepinephrine
D. Hemoglobin

107. **Models are used in science in all of the following ways EXCEPT:**
(Rigorous)

A. Models are crucial for understanding the structure and function of scientific processes
B. Models help us visualize the organs/systems they represent
C. Models create exact replicas of the real items they represent
D. Models are useful for predicting and foreseeing future events such as hurricanes

108. **There are a number of common misconceptions that claim to be based in science. All of the following are misconceptions EXCEPT:**
(Rigorous)

A. Evolution is a process that does not address the origins of life
B. The average person uses only a small fraction of his or her brain
C. Raw sugar causes hyperactive behavior in children
D. Seasons are caused by the Earth's elliptical orbit

109. **One characteristic of electrically charged objects is that any charge is conserved. This means that:**
(Rigorous)

A. Because of the financial cost, electricity should be conserved (saved)
B. A neutral object has no net charge
C. Like charges repel and opposite charges attract
D. None of the above

110. **Which of the following describes a state of balance between opposing forces of change?**
(Easy)

A. Equilibrium
B. Homeostasis
C. Ecological balance
D. All of the above

111. **Which of the following describes the amount of matter in an object?**
(Average)

A. Weight
B. Mass
C. Density
D. Volume

112. **Sound waves are produced by:**
(Easy)

A. Pitch
B. Noise
C. Vibrations
D. Sonar

113. **The Doppler Effect is associated most closely with which property of waves?**
(Average)

A. Amplitude
B. Wavelength
C. Frequency
D. Intensity

114. **The energy of electromagnetic waves is:**
(Rigorous)

A. Radiant energy
B. Acoustical energy
C. Thermal energy
D. Chemical energy

115. **Photosynthesis is the process by which plants make carbohydrates using:**
(Average)

A. The Sun, carbon dioxide, and oxygen
B. The Sun, oxygen, and water
C. Oxygen, water, and carbon dioxide
D. The Sun, carbon dioxide, and water

116. **Identify the correct sequence of organization of living things from lower to higher order:**
(Rigorous)

A. Cell, organelle, organ, tissue, system, organism
B. Cell, tissue, organ, organelle, system, organism
C. Organelle, cell, tissue, organ, system, organism
D. Organelle, tissue, cell, organ, system, organism

117. **What cell organelle contains the cell's stored food?**
(Rigorous)

A. Vacuoles
B. Golgi apparatus
C. Ribosomes
D. Lysosomes

118. **Enzymes speed up reactions by:**
(Rigorous)

A. Utilizing ATP
B. Lowering pH, allowing reaction speed to increase
C. Increasing volume of substrate
D. Lowering energy of activation

119. Which of the following is a correct explanation for scientific *evolution*? *(Rigorous)*

A. Giraffes need to reach higher for leaves to eat, so their necks stretch. The giraffe babies are then born with longer necks. Eventually there are more long-necked giraffes in the population.

B. Giraffes with longer necks are able to reach more leaves, so they eat more and have more babies than other giraffes. Eventually there are more long-necked giraffes in the population.

C. Giraffes want to reach higher for leaves to eat, so they release enzymes into their bloodstream, which in turn causes fetal development of longer-necked giraffes. Eventually there are more long-necked giraffes in the population.

D. Giraffes with long necks are more attractive to other giraffes, so they get the best mating partners and have more babies. Eventually, there are more long-necked giraffes in the population.

120. The theory of seafloor spreading explains: *(Rigorous)*

A. The shapes of the continents
B. How continents collide
C. How continents move apart
D. How continents sink to become part of the ocean floor

121. Weather occurs in which layer of the atmosphere? *(Average)*

A. Troposphere
B. Stratosphere
C. Mesosphere
D. Thermosphere

122. Which of the following types of rock are made from magma? *(Average)*

A. Fossils
B. Sedimentary
C. Metamorphic
D. Igneous

123. **What is the most accurate description of the water cycle?**
(Rigorous)

A. Rain comes from clouds, filling the ocean. The water then evaporates and becomes clouds again.
B. Water circulates from rivers into groundwater and back, while water vapor circulates in the atmosphere.
C. Water is conserved except for chemical or nuclear reactions, and any drop of water could circulate through clouds, rain, groundwater, and surface water.
D. Weather systems cause chemical reactions to break water into its atoms.

124. **Which of the following is the best definition of *meteorite*?**
(Easy)

A. A meteorite is a mineral composed of mica and feldspar
B. A meteorite is material from outer space that has struck the Earth's surface
C. A meteorite is an element that has properties of both metals and nonmetals
D. A meteorite is a very small unit of length measurement

FINE ARTS, HEALTH, AND PHYSICAL EDUCATION

125. **The process of critiquing artwork is:**
(Easy)

A. An asset for all teachers
B. Beyond the scope of the elementary teacher
C. Fairly complex and requires specific training
D. Limited to art historians and professional artists

126. **All of the following are examples of useful art tools for early childhood students EXCEPT:**
(Rigorous)

A. Color wheel
B. Oversized crayons and pencils
C. Fine-tipped brushes
D. Clay

127. **The Renaissance period was concerned with the rediscovery of the works of:**
(Average)

A. Italy
B. Japan
C. Germany
D. Classical Greece and Rome

128. **Which of the following statements is most accurate?**
(Rigorous)

A. Most artists work alone and are rarely affected by the work of other artists
B. Artists in every field are influenced and inspired by the works of others in the various disciplines in the humanities
C. It is rare for visual arts to be influenced by literature or poetry
D. The political climate of an era affects the art of the period only on specific occasions throughout history

129. **A combination of three or more tones sounded at the same time is called a:**
(Average)

A. Harmony
B. Consonance
C. Chord
D. Dissonance

130. **A series of single tones that add up to a recognizable sound is called a:**
(Average)

A. Cadence
B. Rhythm
C. Melody
D. Sequence

131. **The term *conjunto* in music refers to:**
(Average)

A. Two instruments playing at the same time
B. A tempo a little faster than allegro
C. A musical style that involves playing with great feeling
D. A type of Texas-Mexican music

132. **All of the following apply to critiquing music EXCEPT:**
(Rigorous)

A. The keys steps are to listen, analyze, describe, and evaluate
B. Avoid the use of musical terminology in order to facilitate students' enjoyment of music
C. Have students develop their own rubrics for critiques
D. Encourage students to work in pairs

133. **Which of the following is *not* a type of muscle tissue?**
(Easy)

A. Skeletal
B. Cardiac
C. Smooth
D. Fiber

134. **Which of these is a type of joint?**
(Average)

    A. Ball and socket
    B. Hinge
    C. Pivot
    D. All of the above

135. **A physical education instructor anticipates and prevents potential injuries, watches for hidden injuries, and takes an injury evaluation of the entire class. Which of the following strategies to prevent injuries is the teacher demonstrating?**
(Average)

    A. Maintaining hiring standards
    B. Proper use of equipment
    C. Proper procedures for emergencies
    D. Participant screening

136. **All of the following are signs of anorexia nervosa EXCEPT:**
(Average)

    A. Malnutrition
    B. Behavior regression
    C. No outward signs
    D. Recognizable weight loss

137. **Which of the following refers to a muscle's ability to contract over a period of time and maintain strength?**
(Rigorous)

    A. Cardiovascular fitness
    B. Muscle endurance
    C. Muscle fitness
    D. Muscle force

138. **A game of "Simon Says" is an opportunity for the teacher to asses which of the following:**
(Average)

    A. Concept of body awareness
    B. Concept of spatial awareness
    C. Concept of direction and movement
    D. Concept of speed and movement

139. **Bending, stretching, and turning are examples of which type of skill?**
(Average)

    A. Locomotor skills
    B. Nonlocomotor skills
    C. Manipulative skills
    D. Rhythmic skills

140. Which of the following statements is NOT true?
(Rigorous)

   A. Children's motor development and physical fitness are affected by a range of factors, including social, psychological, familial, genetic, and cultural factors

   B. Motor development is complete by the time a student reaches sixth grade

   C. A family's economic status can affect a student's motor development

   D. A physical education program can have a positive impact on a student's level of physical fitness

Answer Key

1.	D	29.	C	57.	C	85.	A	113.	C
2.	D	30.	A	58.	D	86.	A	114.	A
3.	D	31.	B	59.	C	87.	A	115.	D
4.	A	32.	A	60.	A	88.	C	116.	C
5.	C	33.	B	61.	C	89.	C	117.	A
6.	A	34.	D	62.	C	90.	A	118.	D
7.	D	35.	A	63.	C	91.	C	119.	B
8.	C	36.	B	64.	B	92.	D	120.	C
9.	D	37.	C	65.	A	93.	D	121.	A
10.	B	38.	B	66.	B	94.	A	122.	D
11.	A	39.	C	67.	B	95.	D	123.	C
12.	A	40.	D	68.	C	96.	A	124.	B
13.	B	41.	B	69.	D	97.	B	125.	A
14.	A	42.	A	70.	A	98.	B	126.	C
15.	A	43.	C	71.	A	99.	C	127.	D
16.	A	44.	D	72.	C	100.	C	128.	B
17.	B	45.	B	73.	D	101.	B	129.	C
18.	D	46.	D	74.	A	102.	B	130.	C
19.	A	47.	C	75.	B	103.	C	131.	D
20.	D	48.	D	76.	B	104.	A	132.	B
21.	C	49.	C	77.	B	105.	B	133.	D
22.	C	50.	B	78.	D	106.	D	134.	D
23.	A	51.	A	79.	C	107.	C	135.	D
24.	A	52.	A	80.	A	108.	A	136.	C
25.	A	53.	C	81.	C	109.	B	137.	B
26.	D	54.	D	82.	A	110.	D	138.	A
27.	B	55.	C	83.	D	111.	B	139.	B
28.	A	56.	A	84.	B	112.	C	140.	B

Rigor Table

Easy

2, 16, 19, 22, 27, 36, 39, 42, 43, 47, 50, 54, 56, 57, 63, 71, 72, 76, 78, 79, 84, 87, 93, 100, 110, 112, 124, 125, 133

Average

1, 6, 8, 9, 12, 14, 18, 20, 23, 24, 29, 30, 34, 35, 38, 40, 46, 48, 55, 58, 61, 64, 66, 67, 68, 70, 73, 75, 81, 86, 88, 89, 91, 92, 95, 97, 98, 99, 101, 102, 104, 106, 111, 113, 115, 121, 122, 127, 129, 130, 131, 134, 135, 136, 138, 139

Rigorous

3, 4, 5, 7, 10, 11, 13, 15, 17, 21, 25, 26, 28, 31, 32, 33, 37, 41, 44, 45, 49, 51, 52, 53, 59, 60, 62, 65, 69, 74, 77, 80, 82, 83, 85, 90, 94, 96, 103, 105, 107, 108, 109, 114, 116, 117, 118, 119, 120, 123, 126, 128, 132, 137, 140

READING, LANGUAGE, AND LITERATURE

1. While standing in line at the grocery store, three-year-old Megan says to her mother in a regular tone of voice, "Mom, why is that woman so fat?" What does this indicate a lack of understanding of?
    (Average)

    A. Syntax
    B. Semantics
    C. Morphology
    D. Pragmatics

Answer: D. Pragmatics
Pragmatics is the development and understanding of social relevance to conversations and topics. It develops as children age. In this situation Megan simply does not understand, as an adult would, how that question could be viewed as offensive.

2. Oral language development can be enhanced by which of the following?
    (Easy)

    A. Meaningful conversation
    B. Storytelling
    C. Alphabet songs
    D. All of the above

Answer: D. All of the above
Effective oral language development can be encouraged by many different activities including storytelling, rhyming books, meaningful conversation, alphabet songs, dramatic playtime, listening games, and more.

3. **Ms. Chomski is presenting a new story to her class of first graders. In the story, a family visits their grandparents, where they all gather around a record player and listen to music. Many students do not understand what a record player is, especially some children for whom English is not their first language. Which of the following would be best for Ms. Chomski to do?**
(Rigorous)

   A. Discuss what a record player is with her students
   B. Compare a record player with a CD player
   C. Have students look up *record player* in a dictionary
   D. Show the students a picture of a record player

Answer: D. Show the students a picture of a record player
The most effective method for ensuring adequate comprehension is through direct experience. Sometimes this cannot be accomplished and therefore it is necessary to utilize pictures or other visual aids to provide students with experience in another mode besides oral language.

4. **Reading aloud correlates with all of the following EXCEPT:**
(Rigorous)

   A. Reader self-confidence
   B. Better reading comprehension
   C. Literacy development
   D. Overall school success

Answer: A. Reader self-confidence
Reading aloud promotes language acquisition and correlates with literacy development, achieving better reading comprehension, and overall success in school. It may or may not promote reader self-confidence, depending on the reader and his or her skills and personality.

5.   **Mr. Johns is using an activity that involves having students analyze the public speaking of others. All of the following would be guidelines for this activity EXCEPT:**
      (Rigorous)

      A. The speeches to be evaluated are not given by other students
      B. The rubric for evaluating the speeches includes pace, pronunciation, body language, word choice, and visual aids
      C. The speeches to be evaluated are best presented live to give students a more engaging learning experience
      D. One of Mr. John's goals with this activity is to help students improve their own public speaking skills

Answer: C. The speeches to be evaluated are best presented live to give students a more engaging learning experience
Analyzing the speech of others is an excellent technique to help students improve their own public speaking abilities. In most circumstances students cannot view themselves as they give speeches and presentations, so when they get the opportunity to critique, question, and analyze others' speeches, they begin to learn what works and what doesn't work in effective public speaking. However, an important word of warning: *do not* have students critique each other's public speaking skills. It could be very damaging to a student to have his or her peers point out what did not work in a speech. Instead, video is a great tool teachers can use. Any appropriate source of public speaking can be used in the classroom for students to analyze and critique.

6.   **All of the following are true about phonological awareness EXCEPT:**
      (Average)

      A. It may involve print
      B. It is a prerequisite for spelling and phonics
      C. Activities can be done by the children with their eyes closed
      D. It starts before letter recognition is taught

Answer: A. It may involve print
All of the options are aspects of phonological awareness except the first one, A, because phonological awareness does not involve print.

7. **Which of the following explains a significant difference between phonics and phonemic awareness?**
    (Rigorous)

    A. Phonics involves print, while phonemic awareness involves language
    B. Phonics is harder than phonemic awareness
    C. Phonics involves sounds, while phonemic awareness involves letters
    D. Phonics is the application of sounds to print, while phonemic awareness is oral

Answer: D. Phonics is the application of sounds to print, while phonemic awareness is oral
Both phonics and phonemic awareness involve sounds, but it is with phonics that the application of these sounds is applied to print. Phonemic awareness is an oral activity.

8. **Theorist Marilyn Jager Adams, who researches early reading, has outlined five basic types of phonemic awareness tasks. Which of the following is NOT one of the tasks noted by Jager Adams?**
    (Average)

    A. Ability to do oddity tasks
    B. Ability to orally blend words and split syllables
    C. Ability to sound out words when reading aloud
    D. Ability to do phonics manipulation tasks

Answer: C. Ability to sound out words when reading aloud
The tasks Jager Adams has outlined do not include the ability to sound out words when reading aloud. Her five tasks are: 1) The ability to hear rhymes and alliteration, 2) The ability to do oddity tasks (recognize the member of a set that is different, or odd, among the group, 3) The ability to orally blend words and split syllables, 4) The ability to orally segment words, and 5) The ability to do phonics manipulation tasks.

9. **Activities that parents can practice at home to improve phonological and phonemic awareness include which of the following?**
    (Average)

    A. Play games with words that sound alike as you experience them in everyday home activities
    B. Demonstrate how sounds blend together in familiar words
    C. Play a game in which the goal is to find objects with names that begin with a certain initial sound
    D. All of the above

Answer: D. All of the above
Games and demonstrations that help children focus on distinguishing sounds are all useful in improving phonological and phonemic awareness.

10. **The alphabetic principle can best be described by which of the following statements?**
(Rigorous)

A. Most reading skills need to be acquired through a regular teaching of the alphabet
B. Written words are composed of patterns of letters that represent the sounds of spoken words
C. Written words are composed of patterns that must be memorized in order to read well
D. Spoken words (regular and irregular) lead to phonological reading

Answer: B. Written words are composed of patterns of letters that represent the sounds of spoken words
The alphabetic principle is sometimes called graphophonemic awareness. This multi-syllabic technical reading foundation term describes the understanding that written words are composed of patterns of letters that represent the sounds of spoken words. There are basically two parts to the alphabetic principle: 1) An understanding that words are made up of letters and that each letter has a specific sound, 2) The correspondence between sounds and letters leads to phonological reading. This consists of reading regular and irregular words and doing advanced analysis of words.

11. **Which of the following is NOT true about multisensory approaches to teaching the alphabetic principle?**
(Rigorous)

A. Some children can only learn through multisensory techniques
B. Multisensory techniques give multiple cues to enhance memory and learning
C. Quilt book, rhyme time, letter path, and shape game are multisensory strategies
D. Multisensory techniques require direct teaching and ongoing engagement

Answer: A. Some children can only learn through multisensory techniques
Although some children may learn more effectively when multiple senses are involved, there is no evidence to suggest that this is the only way some students can learn. Multisensory techniques do enhance learning and memory and provide more solid grounding when students later learn to apply phonics skills to print. Such activities demand teacher engagement with students to directly teach the concepts related to the alphabetic principle.

12. **Activities that facilitate learning the alphabetic principle include:**
    (Average)

    A. Read alouds, alphabet art, concept books, and name sorts
    B. Read alouds, shared reading, concept books, and picture books
    C. Picture books, concept books, and alphabet books
    D. Alphabet art, name sorts, shared reading, and phonics

Answer: A. Read alouds, alphabet art, concept books, and name sorts
Read alouds, alphabet art, concept books, name sorts, and shared reading are all activities useful to help young children learn the alphabetic principle. Picture books and phonics develop other aspects of reading skills and literacy development.

13. **Which of the following is a convention of print that children learn during reading activities?**
    (Rigorous)

    A. The meaning of words
    B. The left-to-right motion
    C. The purpose of print
    D. The identification of letters

Answer: B. The left-to-right motion
During reading activities, children learn conventions of print. Children learn the way to hold a book, where to begin to read, the left-to-right motion, and how to continue from one line to another.

14. **Alphabet books are classified as:**
    (Average)

    A. Concept books
    B. Easy-to-read books
    C. Board books
    D. Picture books

Answer: A. Concept books
Concept books combine language and pictures to show concrete examples of abstract concepts. One category of concept books is alphabet books, which are popular with children from preschool through grade 2.

15. **To determine an author's purpose, a reader must:**
(Rigorous)

A. Use his or her own judgment
B. Verify all the facts
C. Link the causes to the effects
D. Rely on common sense

Answer: A. Use his or her own judgment
An author may have more than one purpose in writing. Verifying all the facts, linking causes to effects, and relying on common sense can all help a reader in judging the author's purpose, but the reader must use his or her own judgment to determine the author's purpose for writing.

16. **To decode is to:**
(Easy)

A. Construct meaning
B. Sound out a printed sequence of letters
C. Use a special code to decipher a message
D. None of the above

Answer: A. Construct meaning
Word analysis (phonics or decoding) is the process readers use to figure out unfamiliar words based on written patterns. Decoding is the process of constructing the meaning of an unknown word.

17. **Contextual redefinition is a strategy that encourages children to use the context more effectively by presenting them with sufficient vocabulary _____ the reading of a text.**
(Rigorous)

A. after
B. before
C. during
D. none of the above

Answer: B. before
Contextual redefinition is a strategy that encourages children to use the context more effectively by presenting them with sufficient context *before* they begin reading. To apply this strategy, the teacher should first select unfamiliar words for teaching. No more than two or three words should be selected for direct teaching.

18. **What is the best place for students to find appropriate synonyms, antonyms, and other related words to enhance their writing?**
(Average)

   A. Dictionary
   B. Spell check
   C. Encyclopedia
   D. Thesaurus

Answer: D. Thesaurus
Students need plenty of exposure to new words. A thesaurus is an excellent resource to use when writing. Students can use a thesaurus to find appropriate synonyms, antonyms, and other related words to enhance their writing.

19. **Which of the following indicates that a student is a fluent reader?**
(Easy)

   A. Reads texts with expression or prosody
   B. Reads word to word and haltingly
   C. Must intentionally decode a majority of the words
   D. In a writing assignment, sentences are poorly organized structurally

Answer: A. Reads texts with expression or prosody
The teacher should listen to the children read aloud, but there are also clues to reading levels in their writing.

20. **Which of the following reading strategies is NOT associated with fluent reading abilities?**
(Average)

   A. Pronouncing unfamiliar words by finding similarities with familiar words
   B. Establishing a purpose for reading
   C. Formulating questions about the text while reading
   D. Reading sentences word by word

Answer: D. Reading sentences word by word
Pronouncing unfamiliar words by finding similarities with familiar words, establishing a purpose for reading, and formulating questions about the text while reading are all strategies fluent readers use to enhance their comprehension of a text. Reading sentences word by word is a trait of a nonfluent reader. It inhibits comprehension, as the reader focuses on each word separately rather than the meaning of the whole sentence and how it fits into the text.

21. **Automaticity refers to all of the following EXCEPT:**
(Rigorous)

A. Automatic whole-word identification
B. Automatic recognition of syllable types
C. Automatic reactions to the content of a paragraph
D. Automatic identification of graphemes as they relate to four basic word types

Answer: C. Automatic reactions to the content of a paragraph
Automaticity is the ability to automatically recognize words, graphemes, word types, and syllables. This ability progresses through various stages and facilitates reading fluency and prosody. Automaticity is not related to the content of a paragraph or the student's reactions to the content.

22. **Which of the following activities are likely to improve fluency?**
(Easy)

A. Partner reading and a reading theater
B. Phrased reading
C. Both A and B
D. None of the above

Answer: C. Both A and B
Partner reading, tutors, a reading theater, modeling fluent reading, and opportunities for phrased reading are all strategies designed to enhance fluency.

23. **Students are about to read a text that contains words that will need to be understood for the students to understand the text. When should the vocabulary be introduced to students?**
(Average)

A. Before reading
B. During reading
C. After reading
D. It should not be introduced

Answer: A. Before reading
Vocabulary should be introduced before reading if there are words in the text that are necessary for reading comprehension.

24. **Which of the following is an important feature of vocabulary instruction, according to the National Reading Panel?**
(Average)

    A. Repetition of vocabulary items
    B. Keeping a consistent task structure at all times
    C. Teaching vocabulary in more than one language
    D. Isolating vocabulary instruction from other subjects

Answer: A. Repetition of vocabulary items
According to the National Reading Panel, repetition and multiple exposures to vocabulary items are important. Students should be given items that will be likely to appear in many contexts.

25. **A sixth-grade science teacher has given her class a paper to read on the relationship between food and weight gain. The writing contains signal words and phrases such as "because," "consequently," "this is how," and "due to." This paper has which text structure?**
(Rigorous)

    A. Cause and effect
    B. Compare and contrast
    C. Description
    D. Sequencing

Answer: A. Cause and effect
Cause and effect is the relationship between two things when one thing makes something else happen. Writers use this text structure to show order, inform, speculate, and change behavior. This text structure uses the process of identifying potential causes of a problem or issue in an orderly way.

26. **Which of the following is not a strategy of teaching reading comprehension?**
(Rigorous)

    A. Asking questions
    B. Utilizing graphic organizers
    C. Focusing on mental images
    D. Manipulating sounds

Answer: D. Manipulating sounds
Comprehension simply means that the reader can ascribe meaning to text. Teachers can use many strategies to teach comprehension, including questioning, asking students to paraphrase or summarize, utilizing graphic organizers, and focusing on mental images.

27. **The children's literature genre came into its own in the:**
    (Easy)

    A. Seventeenth century
    B. Eighteenth century
    C. Nineteenth century
    D. Twentieth century

Answer: B. Eighteenth century
Children's literature is a genre of its own that emerged as a distinct and independent form in the second half of the eighteenth century. *The Visible World in Pictures,* by John Amos Comenius, a Czech educator, was one of the first printed works and the first picture book.

28. **When evaluating reference sources, students should do all of the following EXCEPT:**
    (Rigorous)

    A. Look for self-published books by the author as evidence of expert status
    B. Examine the level of detail provided by the source
    C. Review the references at the end of the book or article
    D. See if the author presents both sides of an argument or viewpoint

Answer: A. Look for self-published books by the author as evidence of expert status
Anyone can self-publish a book or pamphlet. Experience and background in the subject area have not been reviewed by anyone in many cases. Therefore, more research needs to be done to determine whether a source document is based on reliable, expert information when it has been published by the author.

29. **Graphic organizers:**
    (Average)

    A. are used primarily in grades K-3
    B. work better with poetry than other forms of writing
    C. help readers think critically by pulling out the main idea and supporting details
    D. generally aren't helpful to ELL students

Answer: C. help readers think critically by pulling out the main idea and supporting details
Graphic organizers help readers think critically about an idea, concept, or story by pulling out the main idea and supporting details. These pieces of information can then be depicted graphically through the use of connected geometric shapes. Readers who develop this skill can use it to increase their reading comprehension. Graphic organizers are useful for all ages and types of students, and for many forms for literature and writing.

30. **Which of the following helps students in a way that is similar to using a glossary?**
(Average)

    A. Information in the text such as charts, graphs, maps, diagrams, captions, and photos
    B. Prewriting
    C. Classroom discussion of the main idea
    D. Paired reading

Answer: A. Information in the text such as charts, graphs, maps, diagrams, captions, and photos
Charts, graphs, maps, diagrams, captions, and photos in text can work in the same way as looking up unknown words in the glossary. They can provide more insight into and clarification of concepts and ideas the author is conveying. Students may need to develop these skills to interpret the information accurately, which makes a natural cross-subject opportunity.

31. **Which of these describes the best way to teach spelling?**
(Rigorous)

    A. At the same time that grammar and sentence structure are taught
    B. Within the context of meaningful language experiences
    C. Independently so that students can concentrate on spelling
    D. In short lessons, as students pick up spelling almost immediately

Answer: B. Within the context of meaningful language experiences
Spelling should be taught within the context of meaningful language experiences. Giving a child a list of words to learn to spell and then testing the child on the words every Friday will not aid in the development of spelling. The child must be able to use the words in context and they must have some meaning for the child. The assessment of how well a child can spell or where there are problems also has to be done within a meaningful environment.

32. **Which of the following sentences contains an error in agreement?**
(Rigorous)

    A. Jennifer is one of the women who writes for the magazine.
    B. Each one of their sons plays a different sport.
    C. This band has performed at the Odeum many times.
    D. The data are available online at the listed Web site.

Answer: A. Jennifer is one of the women who writes for the magazine.
Women is the plural subject of the verb. The verb should be *write*.

33. **All of the following are correctly punctuated EXCEPT:**
    (Rigorous)

    A. "The airplane crashed on the runway during takeoff."
    B. I was embarrassed when Ms. White said, "Your slip is showing!"
    C. "The middle school readers were unprepared to understand Bryant's poem 'Thanatopsis.'"
    D. The hall monitor yelled, "Fire! Fire!"

Answer: B. I was embarrassed when Ms. White said, "Your slip is showing!"
B is incorrectly punctuated because in exclamatory sentences, the exclamation point should be positioned outside the closing quotation marks if the quote itself is a statement, command, or cited title. The exclamation point is correctly positioned in choice D because the sentence is declarative but the quotation is an exclamation.

34. **Which of the following is not a technique of prewriting?**
    (Average)

    A. Clustering
    B. Listing
    C. Brainstorming
    D. Proofreading

Answer: D. Proofreading
Proofreading cannot be a method of prewriting because it is done only on texts that have already been written.

35. **Which of the following is NOT a prewriting strategy?**
    (Average)

    A. Analyzing sentences for variety
    B. Keeping an idea book
    C. Writing in a daily journal
    D. Writing down whatever comes to mind

Answer: A. Analyzing sentences for variety
Prewriting strategies assist students in a variety of ways. Common prewriting strategies include keeping an idea book for jotting down ideas, writing in a daily journal, and writing down whatever comes to mind, which is also called "free writing." Analyzing sentences for variety is a revising strategy.

36. **A student has written a paper with the following characteristics: written in first person; characters, setting, and plot; some dialogue; events organized in chronological sequence with some flashbacks. In what genre has the student written?**
(Easy)

    A. Expository writing
    B. Narrative writing
    C. Persuasive writing
    D. Technical writing

Answer: B. Narrative writing
These are all characteristics of narrative writing. Expository writing is intended to give information such as an explanation or directions, and the information is logically organized. Persuasive writing gives an opinion in an attempt to convince the reader that a point of view is valid, or tries to persuade the reader to take a specific action. The goal of technical writing is to clearly communicate particular information to a targeted reader or group of readers.

37. **Exposition occurs within a story:**
(Rigorous)

    A. After the rising action
    B. After the denouement
    C. Before the rising action
    D. Before the setting

Answer: C. Before the rising action
Exposition is where characters and their situations are introduced. *Rising action* is the point at which conflict starts to occur and is often a turning point. *Denouement* is the final resolution of the plot.

38. **Which of the following messages provides the most accessibility to the most learners?**
(Average)

A. Print message
B. Audiovisual message
C. Graphic message
D. Audio message

Answer: B. Audiovisual message
An audiovisual message is the most accessible for learners. It has the advantages of both mediums: the graphic and the audio. Learners' eyes and ears are engaged. Nonreaders get significant access to content. On the other hand, viewing an audiovisual presentation is an even more passive activity than listening to an audio message because information is coming to learners effortlessly through two senses.

39. **Which of the following advertising techniques is based on appealing to our desire to think for ourselves?**
(Easy)

A. Celebrity endorsement
B. Intelligence
C. Independence
D. Lifestyle

Answer: C. Independence
Celebrity endorsements associate product use with a well-known person. Intelligence techniques are based on making consumers feel smart and as if they cannot be fooled. Lifestyle approaches are designed to make us feel we are part of a particular way of living.

40. **Which of the following is NOT useful in creating visual media for the classroom?**
(Average)

A. Limit your graph to just one idea or concept and keep the content simple
B. Balance substance and visual appeal
C. Match the information to the format that will fit it best
D. Make sure to cite all references to copyrighted material

Answer: D. Make sure to cite all references to copyrighted material
Although it may be important to acknowledge copyright and intellectual property ownership of some materials used in visual media, this factor is not a guideline for creating useful visual media for the classroom.

41. **All of the following are examples of ongoing informal assessment techniques used to observe student progress EXCEPT:**
(Rigorous)

   A. Analysis of student work product
   B. Collection of data from assessment tests
   C. Effective questioning
   D. Observation of students

Answer: B. Collection of data from assessment tests
Assessment tests are formal progress-monitoring measures.

42. **Which of the following is a formal reading-level assessment?**
(Easy)

   A. A standardized reading test
   B. A teacher-made reading test
   C. An interview
   D. A reading diary

Answer: A. A standardized reading test
If the assessment is standardized, it has to be objective, whereas B, C, and D are all subjective assessments.

43. **Which of the following is NOT considered a reading level?**
(Easy)

A. Independent
B. Instructional
C. Intentional
D. Frustrational

Answer: C. Intentional
Intentional is not a reading level. Reading levels for the purpose of assessment and planning instruction are as follows:

- *Independent.* This is the level at which the child can read text totally on his or her own. When reading books at the independent level, students will be able to decode between 95 and 100 percent of the words and comprehend the text with 90 percent or better accuracy.
- *Instructional.* This is the level at which the student should be taught because it provides enough difficulty to increase his or her reading skills without providing so much that it becomes too cumbersome to finish the selection. Typically, the acceptable range of accuracy is between 85 and 94 percent, with 75 percent or greater comprehension.
- *Frustrational.* Books at a student's frustrational level are too difficult for the child and should not be used. The frustrational level is any text with less than 85 percent word accuracy and/or less than 75 percent comprehension.

44. **Which of the following are good choices for supporting a thesis?**
(Rigorous)

A. Reasons
B. Examples
C. Answer to the question, "why?"
D. All of the above

Answer: D. All of the above
The correct answer is D. When answering the question "why?" you are giving reasons, but those reasons need to be supported with examples.

45. Which of the following should not be included in the opening paragraph of an informative essay?
(Rigorous)

   A. Thesis sentence
   B. Details and examples supporting the main idea
   C. A broad general introduction to the topic
   D. A style and tone that grabs the reader's attention

Answer: B. Details and examples supporting the main idea
The introductory paragraph should introduce the topic, capture the reader's interest, state the thesis, and prepare the reader for the main points in the essay. Details and examples, however, should be given in the second part of the essay to help develop the thesis.

MATHEMATICS

46. **Which of the following is a true statement regarding manipulatives in mathematics instruction?**
(Average)

A. Manipulatives are materials that students can physically handle
B. Manipulatives help students make concrete concepts abstract
C. Manipulatives include fingers, tiles, paper folding, and ice cream sticks
D. Manipulatives help students make abstract concepts concrete

Answer: D. Manipulatives help students make abstract concepts concrete
Manipulatives are materials that students can physically handle and move, such as fingers and tiles. Manipulatives allow students to understand mathematic concepts by allowing them to see concrete examples of abstract processes. Manipulatives are attractive to students because they appeal to the their visual and tactile senses.

47. **All of the following are tools that can strengthen students' mathematical understanding EXCEPT:**
(Easy)

A. Rulers, scales, and protractors
B. Calculators, counters, and measuring containers
C. Software and hardware
D. Money and software

Answer: C. Software and hardware
Students' understanding of mathematical concepts is strengthened when they use tools to help make the abstract concepts become concrete realities. Teachers have a wide variety of tools available to help students learn mathematics. These include all of the above except for hardware. Hardware technically is not a tool but part of the infrastructure of the classroom.

48. **Which of the following is not a good example of helping students make connections between the real world and mathematics?**
(Average)

   A. Studying a presidential election from the perspective of the math involved
   B. Using weather concepts to teach math
   C. Having student helpers take attendance
   D. Reviewing major mathematical theorems on a regular basis

Answer: D. Reviewing major mathematical theorems on a regular basis
Theorems are abstract math concepts, and reviews, while valuable, are not an example of using everyday events to teach math. Teachers can increase student interest in math by relating mathematical concepts to familiar events in their lives and using real-world examples and data whenever possible. Instead of presenting only abstract concepts and examples, teachers should relate concepts to everyday situations to shift the emphasis from memorization and abstract application to understanding and applied problem solving. This will not only improve students' grasp of math ideas and keep them engaged, it will also help answer the perennial question, "Why do we have to learn math?"

49. **Which of the following is an example of the associative property?**
(Rigorous)

   A. $a (b + c) = ab + bc$
   B. $a + 0 = a$
   C. $(a + b) + c = a + (b + c)$
   D. $a + b = b + a$

Answer: C. $(a + b) + c = a + (b + c)$
The associative property illustrates that the order of addition does not matter. If you first add a and b and then add c to this result, it is the same as if you first add b and c, and then add a to the result.

50. **What is the greatest common factor of 16, 28, and 36?**
(Easy)

   A. 2
   B. 4
   C. 8
   D. 16

Answer: B. 4
The smallest number in this set is 16; its factors are 1, 2, 4, 8, and 16. Sixteen is the largest factor, but it does not divide into 28 or 36. Neither does 8. Four does factor into both 28 and 36.

51. **Mathematical operations are done in the following order:**
(Rigorous)

    A. Simplify inside grouping characters such as parentheses, brackets, square roots, fraction bars, etc.; multiply out expressions with exponents; do multiplication or division, from left to right; do addition or subtraction, from left to right
    B. Do multiplication or division, from left to right; simplify inside grouping characters such as parentheses, brackets, square roots, fraction bars, etc.; multiply out expressions with exponents; do addition or subtraction, from left to right
    C. Simplify inside grouping characters such as parentheses, brackets, square roots, fraction bars, etc.; do addition or subtraction, from left to right; multiply out expressions with exponents; do multiplication or division, from left to right
    D. None of the above

Answer: A. Simplify inside grouping characters such as parentheses, brackets, square roots, fraction bars, etc.; multiply out expressions with exponents; do multiplication or division, from left to right; do addition or subtraction, from left to right
When facing a mathematical problem that requires all mathematical properties to be performed first, you do the math within the parentheses, brackets, square roots, or fraction bars. Then you multiply out expressions with exponents. Next, you do multiplication or division. Finally, you do addition or subtraction.

52. **Which of the following is an irrational number?**
(Rigorous)

    A. .36262626262…
    B. 4
    C. 8.2
    D. -5

Answer: A. .362626262626…
Irrational numbers are numbers that cannot be made into a fraction. This number cannot be made into a fraction.

53. **The number "0" is a member of all of the following groups of numbers EXCEPT:**
(Rigorous)

    A. Whole numbers
    B. Real numbers
    C. Natural numbers
    D. Integers

Answer: C. Natural numbers
The number zero is a whole number, real number, and an integer, but the natural numbers (also known as the counting numbers) start with the number one, not zero.

54. **4,087,361: What number represents the ten thousands' place?**
(Easy)

    A. 4
    B. 6
    C. 0
    D. 8

Answer: D. 8
The ten thousands' place is the number 8 in this problem.

55. **Two mathematics classes have a total of 410 students. The 8:00 a.m. class has 40 more students than the 10:00 a.m. class. How many students are in the 10:00 a.m. class?**
(Average)

    A. 123.3
    B. 370
    C. 185
    D. 330

Answer: C. 185
Let x = the number of students in the 8:00 a.m. class and $x - 40$ = the number of students in the 10:00 a.m. class. So there are 225 students in the 8:00 a.m. class, and $225 - 40 = 185$ in the 10:00 a.m. class, which is Answer C.

56. **Three-dimensional figures in geometry are called:**
    (Easy)

    A. Solids
    B. Cubes
    C. Polygons
    D. Blocks

Answer: A. Solids
Three-dimensional figures are referred to as solids.

57. **The volume is:**
    (Easy)

    A. Area of the faces excluding the bases
    B. Total area of all the faces, including the bases
    C. The number of cubic units in a solid
    D. The measure around the object

Answer: C. The number of cubic units in a solid
Volume refers to how much "stuff" can be placed in a solid. Cubic units are one of many things that can be placed in a solid to measure its volume.

58. **If a right triangle has legs with the measurements of 3 cm and 4 cm, what is the measure of the hypotenuse?**
    (Average)

    A. 6 cm
    B. 1 cm
    C. 7 cm
    D. 5 cm

Answer: D. 5 cm
If you use the Pythagorean Theorem ($a^2 + b^2 = c^2$), you will get 5 cm for the hypotenuse leg. For example: $3^2 + 4^2 = 9 + 16 = 25$. The square root of 25 is 5.

59. **If the radius of a right circular cylinder is doubled, how does its volume change?**
(Rigorous)

    A. No change
    B. Also is doubled
    C. Four times the original
    D. Pi times the original

Answer: C. Four times the original
If the radius of a right circular cylinder is doubled, the volume is multiplied by four because in the formula, the radius is squared. Therefore, the new volume is 2 x 2, or four times the original. The formula for the volume of a cylinder is: $V = \pi r^2 h$

60. **Find the area of a rectangle if you know that the base is 8 cm and the diagonal of the rectangle is 8.5 cm:**
(Rigorous)

    A. 24 cm²
    B. 30 cm²
    C. 18.9 cm²
    D. 24 cm

Answer: A. 24 cm²
The answer is A because the base of the rectangle is also one leg of a right triangle, and the diagonal is the hypotenuse of a triangle. To find the other leg of the triangle, you can use the Pythagorean Theorem. Once you get the other leg of the triangle that is also the height of the rectangle. To get the area, you multiply the base by the height. The reason the answer is A, not D, is because area is measured in centimeters squared, not just centimeters.

61. **An item that sells for $375.00 is put on sale at $120.00. What is the percentage of decrease?**
(Average)

    A. 25%
    B. 28%
    C. 68%
    D. 34%

Answer: C. 68%
In this problem you must set up a cross-multiplication problem. You begin by placing *x*/100 to represent the variable you are solving for over 100%, and then you place 120/375 to represent the new price over the original price. Once you cross-multiply, you get 68, which is the percentage decrease.

62. **What is a translation?**
    (Rigorous)

    A. To turn a figure around a fixed point
    B. When the object has the same shape and same size, but figures face in different directions
    C. To "slide" an object a fixed distance in a given direction
    D. The transformation that "shrinks" or "makes it bigger"

Answer: C. To "slide" an object a fixed distance in a given direction
A translation is when you slide an object a fixed distance but do not change the size of the object.

63. **What measures could be used to report the distance traveled in walking around a track?**
    (Easy)

    A. Degrees
    B. Square meters
    C. Kilometers
    D. Cubic feet

Answer: C. Kilometers
Degrees measure angles; square meters measure area; cubic feet measure volume; and kilometers measure length.

64. **Corporate salaries are listed for several employees. Which would be the best measure of central tendency?**
    (Average)

    $24,000 $24,000 $26,000 $28,000 $30,000 $120,000

    A. Mean
    B. Median
    C. Mode
    D. No difference

Answer: B. Median
The median provides the best measure of central tendency in this case, as the mode is the lowest number and the mean would be disproportionately skewed by the outlier, $120,000.

65.   Given a drawer with 5 black socks, 3 blue socks, and 2 red socks, what is the probability that you will draw two black socks in two draws in a dark room?
(Rigorous)

A. 2/9
B. 1/4
C. 17/18
D. 1/18

Answer: A. 2/9
In this example of conditional probability, the probability of drawing a black sock on the first draw is 5/10. It is implied in the problem that there is no replacement therefore the probability of obtaining a black sock in the second draw is 4/9. Multiply the two probabilities and reduce to lowest terms.

66.   Suppose you have a bag of marbles that contains 2 red marbles, 5 blue marbles, and 3 green marbles. If you replace the first marble chosen, what is the probability you will choose 2 green marbles in a row?
(Average)

A. 2/5
B. 9/100
C. 9/10
D. 3/5

Answer: B. 9/100
When performing a problem in which you replace the item, you multiply the first probability fraction by the second probability fraction and replace the item when finding the second probability.

67.   In probability, the sample space represents:
(Average)

A. An outcome of an experiment
B. A list of all possible outcomes of an experiment
C. The number of times you must flip a coin
D. The amount of room needed to conduct an experiment

Answer: B. A list of all possible outcomes of an experiment
The sample space is the list of all possible outcomes that you can have for an experiment.

68. **Deduction is:**
    (Average)

    A. Logical reasoning
    B. The process of arriving at a conclusion based on other statements that are known to be true
    C. Both A and B
    D. Neither A nor B

Answer: C. Both A and B
Deductive reasoning moves from a generalization or set of examples (such as numbers) to a specific conclusion or solution.

69. **Find the inverse of the following statement: If I like dogs, then I do not like cats.**
    (Rigorous)

    A. If I like dogs, then I do like cats.
    B. If I like cats, then I like dogs.
    C. If I like cats, then I do not like dogs.
    D. If I do not like dogs, then I like cats.

Answer: D. If I do not like dogs, then I like cats.
When you take the inverse of the statement, you negate both statements. By negating both statements you take the opposite of the original statement.

70. **Find the converse of the following statement: If I like math, then I do not like science.**
    (Average)

    A. If I do not like science, then I like math.
    B. If I like math, then I do not like science.
    C. If I do not like math, then I do not like science.
    D. If I like math, then I do not like science.

Answer: A. If I do not like science, then I like math.
When finding the converse of a statement, you take the second part of the statement and reverse it with the first part of the statement. In other words, you reverse the statements.

71. **Which of the following is the basic language of mathematics?**
(Easy)

    A. Symbolic representation
    B. Number lines
    C. Arithmetic operations
    D. Deductive thinking

Answer: A. Symbolic representation
Symbolic representation is the basic language of mathematics. Converting data to symbols allows for easy manipulation and problem solving. Students should have the ability to recognize what the symbolic notation represents and convert information into symbolic form.

72. **The mass of a cookie is closest to:**
(Easy)

    A. 0.5 kg
    B. 0.5 grams
    C. 15 grams
    D. 1.5 grams

Answer: C. 15 grams
A common estimation of mass used in elementary schools is that a paperclip has a mass of approximately one gram, which eliminates choices B and D, as they are very close to 1 gram. A common estimation of one kilogram is equal to one liter of water. Half of one liter of water is still much more than one cookie, eliminating choice A. Therefore, the best estimation for one cookie is narrowed to 15 grams, or choice C.

73. **Using graphics can enhance the presentation of social science information because:**
    (Average)

    A. They can explain complex relationships among various data points
    B. Charts and graphs summarize information well
    C. Maps can describe geographic distribution of historical information
    D. All of the above

Answer: D. All of the above
Social science reporting can be interesting and exciting without graphics, however, visual presentations can aid in bringing the data to life. Any idea presented visually in some manner is easier to understand than simply getting an idea across verbally, by hearing it or reading it.

74. **All of the following are key elements in planning a child-centered curriculum EXCEPT:**
    (Rigorous)

    A. Referring students who need special tutoring
    B. Identifying students' prior knowledge and skills
    C. Sequencing learning activities
    D. Specifying behavioral objectives

Answer: A. Referring students who need special tutoring
Although the referral of students who need specialized services is an ongoing task, it is not a central element of the overall planning and organization of a curriculum. Well-thought-out planning includes specifying behavioral objectives, identifying students' entry behavior (knowledge and skills), selecting and sequencing learning activities to move students from entry behavior to objective, and evaluating the outcomes of instruction in order to improve planning.

75. **The Texas Assessment of Knowledge and Skills (TAKS) test is an example of:**
(Average)

    A. Criterion-referenced assessment
    B. Norm-referenced assessment
    C. Performance-based assessment
    D. Other type of assessment

Answer: B. Norm-referenced assessment
Norm-referenced tests (NRTs) are used to classify student learners for homogenous groupings based on ability levels or basic skills. In many school communities, NRTs are used to classify students into AP (Advanced Placement), honors, regular, or remedial classes that can significantly affect the student's future educational opportunities or success.

TAKS measures statewide curriculum in reading for grades 3-9; writing for grades 4 and 7; English language arts for grades 10 and 11; mathematics for grades 3-11; science for grades 5, 10, and 11, and social studies for grades 8, 10, and 11. The Spanish TAKS is given to grades 3-6. Satisfactory performance on the TAKS at grade 11 is prerequisite for a high-school diploma.

76. **Ms. Gomez has a number of ESL students in her class. In order to meet their specific needs as second-language learners, which of the following would NOT be an appropriate approach?**
(Easy)

    A. Pair students of different ability levels for English practice
    B. Focus most of her instruction on teaching English rather than content
    C. Provide accommodations during testing and with assignments
    D. Use visual aids to help students make word links with familiar objects

Answer: B. Focus most of her instruction on teaching English rather than content
In working with ESOL students, different approaches should be used to ensure that students (a) Get multiple opportunities to learn and practice English, and (b) Still learn content. Content should not be given short shrift or be "dumbed down" for ESOL students.

77. **Which one of the following is NOT a reason why Europeans came to the New World?**
(Rigorous)

A. To find resources in order to increase wealth
B. To establish trade
C. To increase a ruler's power and importance
D. To spread Christianity

Answer: B. To establish trade
The Europeans came to the New World for a number of reasons; they often came to find new natural resources to extract for manufacturing. The Portuguese, Spanish, and English were sent over to increase the monarch's power and to spread influences such as religion (Christianity) and culture. Therefore, the only reason given that Europeans didn't come to the New World was to establish trade.

78. **Which of the following were results of the Age of Exploration?**
(Easy)

A. More complete and accurate maps and charts
B. New and more accurate navigational instruments
C. Proof that the Earth is round
D. All of the above

Answer: D. All of the above
The importance of the Age of Exploration was not only the discovery and colonization of the New World, but also better maps and charts; new accurate navigational instruments; increased knowledge; great wealth; new and different foods and items not known in Europe; a new hemisphere as a refuge from poverty and persecution, and as a place to start a new and better life; and proof that Asia could be reached by sea and that the Earth was round; ships and sailors would not sail off the edge of a flat Earth and disappear forever into nothingness.

79. **The belief that the United States should control all of North America was called:**
(Easy)

A. Westward expansion
B. Pan Americanism
C. Manifest Destiny
D. Nationalism

Answer: C. Manifest Destiny
The belief that the United States should control all of North America was called Manifest Destiny. This idea fueled much of the violence and aggression toward those already occupying the lands such as the Native Americans. Manifest Destiny was certainly driven by sentiments of (D) nationalism and gave rise to (A) westward expansion.

80. **Nationalism can be defined as the division of land and resources according to which of the following?**
(Rigorous)

A. Religion, race, or political ideology
B. Religion, race, or gender
C. Historical boundaries, religion, or race
D. Race, gender, or political ideology

Answer: A. Religion, race, or political ideology
Religion, race, and political ideology are some of the characteristics that determine national entity. Tribal membership, language, ethnic affiliation, and even treaty demarcations can dictate national boundaries. Historical boundaries may contribute to conflicts among people but they are generally secondary to another affiliation. To date, gender has not been a determining factor, although the treatment of women, for example, may be a contributing factor in some nationalistic conflicts.

81. **The study of the social behavior of minority groups would be in the area of:**
(Average)

A. Anthropology
B. Psychology
C. Sociology
D. Cultural geography

Answer: C. Sociology
The study of social behavior in minority groups would be primarily in the area of sociology, as it is the discipline most concerned with social interaction. However, it could be argued that anthropology, psychology, and cultural geography would have some interest in the study of social behavior as well.

82. **"Participant observation" is a method of study most closely associated with and used in:**
    (Rigorous)

    A. Anthropology
    B. Archaeology
    C. Sociology
    D. Political science

Answer: A. Anthropology
"Participant observation" is a method of study most closely associated with and used in anthropology, the study of human cultures. Archaeologists typically study the remains of people, animals, or other physical things. Sociology is the study of human society and usually involves surveys, controlled experiments, and field studies. Political science is the study of political life, including justice, freedom, power, and equality, using a variety of methods.

83. **For the historian studying ancient Egypt, which of the following would be least useful?**
    (Rigorous)

    A. The record of an ancient Greek historian on Greek-Egyptian interaction
    B. Letters from an Egyptian ruler to his/her regional governors
    C. Inscriptions on stele of the fourteenth Egyptian dynasty
    D. Letters from a nineteenth-century Egyptologist to his wife

Answer: D. Letters from a nineteenth-century Egyptologist to his wife
Historians use primary sources from the actual time they are studying whenever possible. Ancient Greek records of interaction with Egypt, letters from an Egyptian ruler to regional governors, and inscriptions from the fourteenth Egyptian dynasty are all primary sources created at or near the actual time being studied. Letters from a nineteenth-century Egyptologist would not be considered primary sources, as they were created thousands of years after the time period being studied and may not even be about the subject being studied.

84. **The term *sectionalism* refers to:**
    (Easy)

    A. Different regions of the continent
    B. Issues between the North and South
    C. Different regions of the country
    D. Different groups of countries

Answer: B. Issues between the North and South
The term *sectionalism* referred to slavery and related issues before the Civil War. The Southern economy was agricultural and used slave labor. The North was antislavery and industrial.

85. **Which political group pushed the Reconstruction measures through Congress after Lincoln's death?**
    (Rigorous)

    A. The Radical Republicans
    B. The Radical Democrats
    C. The Whigs
    D. The Independents

Answer: A. The Radical Republicans
In 1866, the Radical Republicans won control of Congress and passed the Reconstruction Acts, which placed the governments of the southern states under the control of the federal military. With this backing, the Republicans began to implement their policies such as granting all black men the vote and denying the vote to former Confederate soldiers. Congress had passed the Thirteenth, Fourteenth, and Fifteenth Amendments, granting citizenship and civil rights to blacks. Ratification of these amendments was a condition of readmission into the Union by the rebel states.

86. **As a result of the Missouri Compromise:**
    (Average)

    A. Slavery was not allowed in the Louisiana Purchase
    B. The Louisiana Purchase was nullified
    C. Louisiana separated from the Union
    D. The Embargo Act was repealed

Answer: A. Slavery was not allowed in the Louisiana Purchase
The Missouri Compromise was the agreement that eventually allowed Missouri to enter the Union. It did not nullify the Louisiana Purchase or the Embargo Act or separate Louisiana from the Union. As a result of the Missouri Compromise, slavery was specifically banned north of the boundary 36° 30'.

87.	**Which country was a cold war foe of the United States?**
	(Easy)

	A. Soviet Union
	B. Brazil
	C. Canada
	D. Argentina

Answer: A. Soviet Union
The Soviet Union was a cold war superpower and foe of the United States in its determination to fight the spread of Communism.

88.	**The international organization established to work for world peace at the end of the Second World War was the:**
	(Average)

	A. League of Nations
	B. United Federation of Nations
	C. United Nations
	D. United World League

Answer: C. United Nations
The international organization established to work for world peace at the end of the Second World War was the United Nations. From the ashes of the failed League of Nations, established following World War I, the United Nations continues to be a major player in world affairs today.

89.	**What event triggered World War I?**
	(Average)

	A. The fall of the Weimar Republic
	B. The resignation of the czar
	C. The assassination of Austrian Archduke Ferdinand
	D. The assassination of the czar

Answer: C. The assassination of Austrian Archduke Ferdinand
There were regional conflicts and feelings of intense nationalism prior to the outbreak of World War I. The precipitating factor was the assassination of Austrian Archduke Ferdinand and his wife while they were in Sarajevo, Serbia.

90. **What is the most significant environmental change in Texas over the last century?**
(Rigorous)

    A. The number of square miles devoted to living space
    B. Continued exploration for oil and gas
    C. Development along the Gulf Coast
    D. Changes in agricultural practices

Answer: A. The number of square miles devoted to living space
The most drastic change to the environment wrought by people has been the sheer number of square miles devoted to living space. Texas still maintains vast areas of agricultural and ranch land, but that number is shrinking by the year, as more and more people claim and put stakes down on land designed to be lived on exclusively. The farmers of the past lived on their land but also lived off it. Their houses were part of their farms and their jobs were working the land. Nowadays, skyscrapers dot the skylines of large cities along with high-rise apartment buildings, which serve the sole function of providing living areas for the people who work in the large cities.

91. **The end to hunting, gathering, and fishing of prehistoric people was due to:**
(Average)

    A. Domestication of animals
    B. Building crude huts and houses
    C. Development of agriculture
    D. Organized government in villages

Answer: C. Development of agriculture
Although the domestication of animals, the building of huts and houses, and the first organized governments were all important steps made by early civilizations, it was the development of agriculture that ended the once-dominant practices of hunting, gathering, and fishing among prehistoric people. The development of agriculture provided a more efficient use of time and, for the first time, a surplus of food. This greatly improved the quality of life and contributed to early population growth.

92. **Which of the following is most useful in showing differences in variables at a specific point in time?**
(Average)

A. Histogram
B. Scatter plots
C. Pie chart
D. Bar graph

Answer: D. Bar graph
Bar graphs are simple and basic, showing a difference in variables at a specific point in time. Histograms are good for summarizing large sets of data in intervals. Pie charts show proportions, and scatter plots demonstrate correlations, or relationships between variables.

93. **Capitalism and communism are alike in that they are both:**
(Easy)

A. Organic systems
B. Political systems
C. Centrally planned systems
D. Economic systems

Answer: D. Economic systems
While economic and political systems are often closely connected, capitalism and communism are primarily economic systems. Capitalism is a system of economics that allows the open market to determine the relative value of goods and services. Communism is an economic system in which the market is planned by a central state. While communism is a centrally planned system, this is not true of capitalism. Organic systems are studied in biology, a natural science.

94. **During the 1920s, the United States almost completely stopped all immigration. One of the reasons was:**
(Rigorous)

A. Plentiful, cheap unskilled labor was no longer needed by industrialists
B. War debts from World War I made it difficult to render financial assistance
C. European nations were reluctant to allow people to leave since there was a need to rebuild populations and economic stability
D. The United States did not become a member of the League of Nations

Answer: A. Plentiful, cheap unskilled labor was no longer needed by industrialists
The United States almost completely stopped all immigration during the 1920s because their once much-needed cheap, unskilled labor jobs, made available by the once-booming industrial economy, were no longer needed. This had much to do with the increased use of machines to do the work once done by cheap, unskilled laborers.

95. **In the 1800s, the era of industrialization and growth was characterized by:**
    (Average)

    A. Small firms
    B. Public ownership
    C. Worker-owned enterprises
    D. Monopolies and trusts

Answer: D. Monopolies and trusts
The era of industrialization and business expansion was characterized by big businesses and monopolies that merged into trusts. There were few small firms and there was no public ownership or worker-owned enterprises.

96. **Which one of the following would NOT be considered a result of World War II?**
    (Rigorous)

    A. Economic depressions and slow resumption of trade and financial aid
    B. Western Europe was no longer the center of world power
    C. The beginnings of new power struggles, not only in Europe but in Asia as well
    D. Territorial and boundary changes for many nations, especially in Europe

Answer: A. Economic depressions and slow resumption of trade and financial aid
Following World War II, the economy was vibrant and flourished from the stimulus of war and the world's increased dependence on U.S. industries. Therefore, World War II didn't result in economic depressions and slow resumption of trade and financial aid. Western Europe was no longer the center of world power. New power struggles arose in Europe and Asia, and many European nations experienced changing territories and boundaries.

97. **The New Deal was:**
    (Average)

    A. A trade deal with England
    B. A series of programs to provide relief during the Great Depression
    C. A new exchange rate regime
    D. A plan for tax relief

Answer: B. A series of programs to provide relief during the Great Depression
The New Deal consisted of a myriad of different programs aimed at providing relief during the Great Depression. Many of the programs were public works programs building bridges, roads, and other infrastructure.

98. **Which of the following is an example of a direct democracy?**
(Average)

   A. Elected representatives
   B. Greek city-states
   C. The Constitution
   D. The Confederate states

Answer: B. Greek city-states
The Greek city-states are an example of a direct democracy, as their leaders were elected directly by the citizens, and the citizens themselves were given voice in government.

99. **Many governments in Europe today have which of the following type of government?**
(Average)

   A. Absolute monarchies
   B. Constitutional governments
   C. Constitutional monarchies
   D. Another form of government

Answer: C. Constitutional monarchies
Over the centuries absolute monarchies were modified, and constitutional monarchies emerged. This form of government recognizes a monarch as leader but invests most of the legal authority in a legislative body such as a Parliament.

SCIENCE

100. **Accepted procedures for preparing solutions include the use of:**
(Easy)

   A. Alcohol
   B. Hydrochloric acid
   C. Distilled water
   D. Tap water

Answer: C. Distilled water
Alcohol and hydrochloric acid should never be used to make solutions unless one is instructed to do so. All solutions should be made with distilled water because tap water contains dissolved particles that can affect the results of an experiment.

101. **Laboratory activities contribute to student performance in all of the following domains EXCEPT:**
(Average)

    A. Process skills such as observing and measuring
    B. Memorization skills
    C. Analytical skills
    D. Communication skills

Answer: B. Memorization skills
Laboratory activities develop a wide variety of investigative, organizational, creative, and communicative skills. The laboratory provides an optimal setting for motivating students while they experience what science is. Such learning opportunities are not focused on memorization but on critical thinking and doing. Laboratory activities enhance student performance in the following domains:

- Process skills: observing, measuring, and manipulating physical objects
- Analytical skills: reasoning, deduction, and critical thinking
- Communication skills: organizing information and writing
- Conceptualization of scientific phenomena

102. **Which is the correct order of methodology?**
(Average)

    1. Collecting data.
    2. Planning a controlled experiment.
    3. Drawing a conclusion.
    4. Hypothesizing a result.
    5. Revisiting a hypothesis to answer a question.

    A. 1, 2, 3, 4, 5
    B. 4, 2, 1, 3, 5
    C. 4, 5, 1, 3, 2
    D. 1, 3, 4, 5, 2

Answer: B. 4, 2, 1, 3, 5
The correct methodology for the scientific method is first to make a meaningful hypothesis (educated guess) and then to plan and execute a controlled experiment to test that hypothesis. Using the data collected in the experiment, the scientist then draws conclusions and attempts to answer the original question related to the hypothesis.

103. **In an experiment measuring the growth of bacteria at different temperatures, what is the independent variable?**
(Rigorous)

A. Number of bacteria
B. Growth rate of bacteria
C. Temperature
D. Size of bacteria

Answer: C. Temperature
To answer this question, recall that the independent variable in an experiment is the entity that the scientist changes in order to observe the effects, or the dependent variable(s). In this experiment, temperature is changed in order to measure growth of bacteria, so (C) is the answer. Note that choice (A) is the dependent variable and that neither (B) nor (D) is directly relevant to the question.

104. **Which of the following is a misconception about the task of teaching science in elementary school?**
(Average)

A. Teach facts as a priority over teaching how to solve problems
B. Involve as many senses as possible in the learning experience
C. Accommodate individual differences in pupils' learning styles
D. Consider the effect of technology on people rather than on material things

Answer: A. Teach facts as a priority over teaching how to solve problems
Prioritizing facts over problem solving is a common misconception in elementary schools. Often, teachers focus on requiring students to learn and recall facts and information alone, rather than teaching them how to apply the learned facts in solving real scientific problems. In fact, problem solving is a vital skill that students need to learn and utilize in all classroom settings, as well as in the real world. Choices B, C, and D all describe effective teaching strategies that exceptional teachers use in their science classrooms.

105. **Which of the following is the most accurate definition of a nonrenewable resource?**
    (Rigorous)

    A. A nonrenewable resource is never replaced once used
    B. A nonrenewable resource is replaced on a time scale that is very long relative to human life spans
    C. A nonrenewable resource is a resource that can only be manufactured by humans
    D. A nonrenewable resource is a species that has already become extinct

Answer: B. A nonrenewable resource is replaced on a time scale that is very long relative to human life spans
Renewable resources are renewed, or replaced, in time for humans to use more of them. Examples include fast-growing plants, animals, and oxygen gas. (Note that while sunlight is often considered a renewable resource, it is actually a nonrenewable but extremely abundant resource.) Nonrenewable resources renew themselves only on very long time scales, usually geologic time scales. Examples include minerals, metals, and fossil fuels.

106. **All of the following are hormones in the human body EXCEPT:**
    (Average)

    A. Cortisol
    B. Testosterone
    C. Norepinephrine
    D. Hemoglobin

Answer: D. Hemoglobin
Hemoglobin refers to red blood cells. Cortisol and norepinephrine are stress-related hormones. Testosterone is a sex-related hormone.

107. **Models are used in science in all of the following ways EXCEPT:**
    (Rigorous)

    A. Models are crucial for understanding the structure and function of scientific processes
    B. Models help us visualize the organs/systems they represent
    C. Models create exact replicas of the real items they represent
    D. Models are useful for predicting and foreseeing future events such as hurricanes

Answer: C. Models create exact replicas of the real items they represent.
One of the limitations of models is that they *cannot* be exact replicas of real objects or processes. However, they are very useful for conceptualization, visualization, and prediction.

108. **There are a number of common misconceptions that claim to be based in science. All of the following are misconceptions EXCEPT:** *(Rigorous)*

   A. Evolution is a process that does not address the origins of life
   B. The average person uses only a small fraction of his or her brain
   C. Raw sugar causes hyperactive behavior in children
   D. Seasons are caused by the Earth's elliptical orbit

Answer: A. Evolution is a process that does not address the origins of life
The theory of evolution presupposes existing life, but does not explain the *origins* of life. This is a good example of a truth that can easily be misconstrued. Most people holding misconceptions are not aware that their beliefs are erroneous. It is critical that instructors understand common misconceptions in science so that they can not only avoid them but also correct them. Some of the most common misconceptions are derived from imprecise language—students often do not understand scientific terminology very well and words with precise scientific meaning are sometimes interpreted in a nonscientific, more general way. Also, media reporting on scientific subjects (particularly politically sensitive issues or popular science topics) is sometimes inaccurate or speculative. Finally, widely held public opinions of scientific topics are often incorrect or only partially correct.

109. **One characteristic of electrically charged objects is that any charge is conserved. This means that:** *(Rigorous)*

   A. Because of the financial cost, electricity should be conserved (saved)
   B. A neutral object has no net charge
   C. Like charges repel and opposite charges attract
   D. None of the above

Answer: B. A neutral object has no net charge
A plastic rod that is rubbed with fur will become electrically charged and will attract small pieces of paper. The charge on the plastic rod rubbed with fur is negative. If the plastic rod and fur are initially neutral, when the fur charges the rod a negative charge is transferred from the fur to the rod. The net negative charge on the rod is equal to the net positive charge on the fur. This is an example of the charge being conserved.

110. **Which of the following describes a state of balance between opposing forces of change?**
(Easy)

   A. Equilibrium
   B. Homeostasis
   C. Ecological balance
   D. All of the above

Answer: D. All of the above
Homeostasis and ecological balance are specific examples of equilibrium, a state of balance between opposing forces of change.

111. **Which of the following describes the amount of matter in an object?**
(Average)

   A. Weight
   B. Mass
   C. Density
   D. Volume

Answer: B. Mass
Mass is a measure of the amount of matter in an object. Two objects of equal mass will balance each other on a simple balance scale, no matter where the scale is located. For instance, two rocks with the same mass that are in balance on Earth will also be in balance on the Moon. They will feel heavier on Earth than on the Moon because of the gravitational pull of the Earth. So, although the two rocks have the same mass, they will have different weight. Weight is the measure of the Earth's pull of gravity on an object. It can also be defined as the pull of gravity between other bodies. Volume is the amount of cubic space an object occupies, and density is the mass of a substance per unit of volume.

112. **Sound waves are produced by:**
(Easy)

A. Pitch
B. Noise
C. Vibrations
D. Sonar

Answer: C. Vibrations
Sound waves are produced by a vibrating body. The vibrating object moves forward and compresses the air in front of it; it then reverses direction so pressure on the air decreases and the air molecules expand. The vibrating air molecules move back and forth, parallel to the direction of motion of the wave as they pass the energy from adjacent air molecules closer to the source to air molecules farther away from the source.

113. **The Doppler effect is associated most closely with which property of waves?**
(Average)

A. Amplitude
B. Wavelength
C. Frequency
D. Intensity

Answer: C. Frequency
The Doppler effect accounts for an apparent increase in frequency when a wave source moves toward a wave receiver or apparent decrease in frequency when a wave source moves away from a wave receiver. (Note that the receiver could also be moving toward or away from the source.) As the wave fronts are released, motion toward the receiver mimics more frequent wave fronts, while motion away from the receiver mimics less frequent wave fronts. Meanwhile, the amplitude, wavelength, and intensity of the wave are not as relevant to this process (although moving closer to a wave source makes it seem more intense).

114. **The energy of electromagnetic waves is:**
    (Rigorous)

    A. Radiant energy
    B. Acoustical energy
    C. Thermal energy
    D. Chemical energy

Answer: A. Radiant energy
Radiant energy is the energy of electromagnetic waves. Light, visible and otherwise, is an example of radiant energy. Acoustical energy, or sound energy, is the movement of energy through an object in waves. Energy that forces an object to vibrate creates sound. Thermal energy is the total internal energy of objects created by the vibration and movement of atoms and molecules. Heat is the transfer of thermal energy. Chemical energy is the energy stored in the chemical bonds of molecules. For example, the energy derived from gasoline is chemical energy. Other forms of energy include electrical, mechanical, and nuclear energy.

115. **Photosynthesis is the process by which plants make carbohydrates using:**
    (Average)

    A. The Sun, carbon dioxide, and oxygen
    B. The Sun, oxygen, and water
    C. Oxygen, water, and carbon dioxide
    D. The Sun, carbon dioxide, and water

Answer: D. The Sun, carbon dioxide, and water
Photosynthesis requires the energy of the Sun, carbon dioxide, and water. Oxygen is a waste product of photosynthesis.

116. **Identify the correct sequence of organization of living things from lower to higher order:**
    (Rigorous)

    A. Cell, organelle, organ, tissue, system, organism
    B. Cell, tissue, organ, organelle, system, organism
    C. Organelle, cell, tissue, organ, system, organism
    D. Organelle, tissue, cell, organ, system, organism

Answer: C. Organelle, cell, tissue, organ, system, organism
Organelles are parts of the cell; cells make up tissue, which makes up organs. Organs work together in systems (e.g., the respiratory system), and the organism is the living thing as a whole.

117. **What cell organelle contains the cell's stored food?**
   (Rigorous)

   A. Vacuoles
   B. Golgi apparatus
   C. Ribosomes
   D. Lysosomes

Answer: A. Vacuoles
In a cell, the subparts are called organelles. Of these, the vacuoles hold stored food (and water and pigments). The Golgi apparatus sorts molecules from other parts of the cell; the ribosomes are sites of protein synthesis; and the lysosomes contain digestive enzymes.

118. **Enzymes speed up reactions by:**
   (Rigorous)

   A. Utilizing ATP
   B. Lowering pH, allowing reaction speed to increase
   C. Increasing volume of substrate
   D. Lowering energy of activation

Answer: D. Lowering energy of activation
Because enzymes are catalysts, they work the same way: They cause the formation of activated chemical complexes, which require a lower activation energy. Therefore, the answer is D. ATP is an energy source for cells, and pH or volume changes may or may not affect reaction rate, so these choices can be eliminated.

119. **Which of the following is a correct explanation for scientific *evolution*?** *(Rigorous)*

A. Giraffes need to reach higher for leaves to eat, so their necks stretch. The giraffe babies are then born with longer necks. Eventually there are more long-necked giraffes in the population.
B. Giraffes with longer necks are able to reach more leaves, so they eat more and have more babies than other giraffes. Eventually there are more long-necked giraffes in the population.
C. Giraffes want to reach higher for leaves to eat, so they release enzymes into their bloodstream, which in turn causes fetal development of longer-necked giraffes. Eventually there are more long-necked giraffes in the population.
D. Giraffes with long necks are more attractive to other giraffes, so they get the best mating partners and have more babies. Eventually, there are more long-necked giraffes in the population.

Answer: B. Giraffes with longer necks are able to reach more leaves, so they eat more and have more babies than other giraffes. Eventually, there are more long-necked giraffes in the population.
Organisms with a life/reproductive advantage produce more offspring. Over many generations, this changes the proportions of the population. In any case, it is impossible for a stretched neck (A) or a fervent desire (C) to result in a biologically mutated baby. Although there are traits that are naturally selected because of mate attractiveness and fitness (D), this is not the primary situation here, so choice B is the answer.

120. **The theory of seafloor spreading explains:** *(Rigorous)*

A. The shapes of the continents
B. How continents collide
C. How continents move apart
D. How continents sink to become part of the ocean floor

Answer: C. How continents move apart
In the theory of seafloor spreading, the movement of the ocean floor causes continents to spread apart from one another. This occurs because crust plates split apart, and new material is added to the plate edges. This process pulls the continents apart, or it may create new separations and is believed to have caused the formation of the Atlantic Ocean.

121. **Weather occurs in which layer of the atmosphere?**
(Average)

    A. Troposphere
    B. Stratosphere
    C. Mesosphere
    D. Thermosphere

Answer: A. Troposphere
The atmosphere is divided into four main layers based on temperature. The troposphere is the layer closest to the Earth's surface and all weather phenomena occur here, as it is the layer with the most water vapor and dust. Air temperature decreases with increasing altitude. The average thickness is 7 miles (11 km).

The stratosphere is a layer that contains very little water so clouds in this layer are very rare. The ozone layer is located in the upper portions of the stratosphere. Air temperature is fairly constant but does increase somewhat with height due to the absorption of solar energy and ultraviolet rays from the ozone layer.

Air temperature decreases with height again in the mesosphere, which is the coldest layer, with temperatures in the range of -100°C at the top. The thermosphere extends upward into space. Oxygen molecules in this layer absorb energy from the Sun, causing temperatures to increase with height.

122. **Which of the following types of rock are made from magma?**
(Average)

    A. Fossils
    B. Sedimentary
    C. Metamorphic
    D. Igneous

Answer: D. Igneous
Metamorphic rocks are formed by high temperatures and great pressures. Fluid sediments are transformed into solid sedimentary rocks. Only igneous rocks are formed from magma.

123. **What is the most accurate description of the water cycle?**
    (Rigorous)

    A. Rain comes from clouds, filling the ocean. The water then evaporates and becomes clouds again.
    B. Water circulates from rivers into groundwater and back, while water vapor circulates in the atmosphere.
    C. Water is conserved except for chemical or nuclear reactions, and any drop of water could circulate through clouds, rain, groundwater, and surface water.
    D. Weather systems cause chemical reactions to break water into its atoms.

Answer: C. Water is conserved except for chemical or nuclear reactions, and any drop of water could circulate through clouds, rain, groundwater, and surface water.
All natural chemical cycles, including the water cycle, depend on the principle of conservation of mass. Any drop of water may circulate through the hydrologic system, ending up in a cloud, as rain, or as surface or groundwater. Although choices A and B describe parts of the water cycle, the most comprehensive answer is C.

124. **Which of the following is the best definition of *meteorite*?**
    (Easy)

    A. A meteorite is a mineral composed of mica and feldspar
    B. A meteorite is material from outer space that has struck the Earth's surface
    C. A meteorite is an element that has properties of both metals and nonmetals
    D. A meteorite is a very small unit of length measurement

Answer: B. A meteorite is material from outer space that has struck the Earth's surface
Meteoroids are pieces of matter in space, composed of particles of rock and metal. If a meteoroid travels through the Earth's atmosphere, friction causes burning and a "shooting star" or meteor. If the meteor strikes the Earth's surface, it is known as a meteorite. Note that although the suffix *-ite* often means a mineral, choice A is incorrect. Choice C refers to a metalloid rather than a meteorite, and choice D is simply a misleading pun on *meter*.

FINE ARTS, HEALTH, AND PHYSICAL EDUCATION

125. **The process of critiquing artwork is:**
    (Easy)

    A. An asset for all teachers
    B. Beyond the scope of the elementary teacher
    C. Fairly complex and requires specific training
    D. Limited to art historians and professional artists

Answer: A. An asset for all teachers
The elementary teacher's ability to think critically and problem-solve is reflected in her or his teaching in many ways, including the way art is perceived and discussed in the classroom. The capacity to critique a work of art is an asset for all teachers, especially in classrooms with integrated curricula, where art is taught in conjunction with other subjects, or in classrooms where there is no separate art program. Many people in various settings can learn to critique art.

126. **All of the following are examples of useful art tools for early childhood students EXCEPT:**
    (Rigorous)

    A. Color wheel
    B. Oversized crayons and pencils
    C. Fine-tipped brushes
    D. Clay

Answer: C. Fine-tipped brushes
Many prekindergarten and kindergarten students use oversized pencils and crayons for the first semester. Typically, after this first semester children gradually develop the ability to use smaller-sized materials. However, they usually do not use fine-tipped brushes until the middle grades due to the lack of adequate fine-motor skills. The color wheel is an excellent lesson for young children, and students begin to learn the uses of primary and secondary colors. Clay is also a valuable medium for children; it offers many opportunities for learning about texture, shape, line, and form as well as a good opportunity to be creatively expressive.

127. **The Renaissance period was concerned with the rediscovery of the works of:**
(Average)

A. Italy
B. Japan
C. Germany
D. Classical Greece and Rome

Answer: D. Classical Greece and Rome

The Renaissance period was concerned with the rediscovery of the works of classical Greece and Rome. The art, literature, and architecture of this period (ca. 1400-1630 CE) were inspired by classical order and style, which tended to be formal, simple, and concerned with the ideal human proportions.

128. **Which of the following statements is most accurate?**
(Rigorous)

A. Most artists work alone and are rarely affected by the work of other artists
B. Artists in every field are influenced and inspired by the works of others in the various disciplines in the humanities
C. It is rare for visual arts to be influenced by literature or poetry
D. The political climate of an era affects the art of the period only on specific occasions throughout history

Answer: B. Artists in every field are influenced and inspired by the works of others in the various disciplines in the humanities

The history of the humanities is replete with examples of artists in every field being influenced and inspired by specific works of others. Influence and inspiration continuously cross the lines between the various disciples in the humanities.

129. **A combination of three or more tones sounded at the same time is called a:**
(Average)

A. Harmony
B. Consonance
C. Chord
D. Dissonance

Answer: C. Chord

A chord is three or more tones combined and sounded simultaneously. Dissonance is the simultaneous sounding of tones that produce a feeling of tension or unrest and a feeling that further resolution is needed. Harmony is the sound resulting from the simultaneous sounding of two or more tones consonant with one another.

130. **A series of single tones that add up to a recognizable sound is called a:**
(Average)

A. Cadence
B. Rhythm
C. Melody
D. Sequence

Answer: C. Melody
A melody is an arrangement of single tones in a meaningful sequence. Cadence is the closing of a phrase or section of music. Rhythm is the regular occurrence of accented beats that shape the character of music or dance.

131. **The term *conjunto* in music refers to:**
(Average)

A. Two instruments playing at the same time
B. A tempo a little faster than allegro
C. A musical style that involves playing with great feeling
D. A type of Texas-Mexican music

Answer: D. A type of Texas-Mexican music
Around the turn of the century in Texas, another clash of cultures produced the Texas-Mexican music called *conjunto*. Working-class musicians from German and Mexican backgrounds combined their talents to produce this folk music, which used the accordion as its main instrument. Musicians could easily transport accordions, making them the perfect accompaniment for dancing, eating, gambling, and other social events.

132. **All of the following apply to critiquing music EXCEPT:**
(Rigorous)

A. The keys steps are to listen, analyze, describe, and evaluate
B. Avoid the use of musical terminology in order to facilitate students' enjoyment of music
C. Have students develop their own rubrics for critiques
D. Encourage students to work in pairs

Answer: B. Avoid the use of musical terminology in order to facilitate students' enjoyment of music
Teaching basic music terminology is a prerequisite for any critique process. Without the necessary language, it is not effective to try to evaluate a piece of music. Similarly, students must be given the opportunity to develop listening skills so they are able to hear different musical elements, themes, instruments, and tones. They will also benefit from an overview of the sounds of different instruments and a listing of musical styles.

133. **Which of the following is *not* a type of muscle tissue?**
    (Easy)

    A. Skeletal
    B. Cardiac
    C. Smooth
    D. Fiber

Answer: D. Fiber
The main function of the muscular system is movement. There are three types of muscle tissue: skeletal, cardiac, and smooth. Fiber is unrelated to muscle.

134. **Which of these is a type of joint?**
    (Average)

    A. Ball and socket
    B. Hinge
    C. Pivot
    D. All of the above

Answer: D. All of the above
A joint is where two bones meet. Joints enable movement. Hinge, ball and socket, and pivot are types of joints.

135. **A physical education instructor anticipates and prevents potential injuries, watches for hidden injuries, and takes an injury evaluation of the entire class. Which of the following strategies to prevent injuries is the teacher demonstrating?**
    (Average)

    A. Maintaining hiring standards
    B. Proper use of equipment
    C. Proper procedures for emergencies
    D. Participant screening

Answer: D. Participant screening
In order for the instructor to know each student's physical status, he or she takes an injury evaluation. Such surveys are one way to know the physical status of an individual. Injury evaluations chronicle past injuries, tattoos, activities, and diseases an individual may have or have had. It helps the instructor know the limitations of each individual. Participant screening covers all forms of surveying and anticipation of injuries.

136. **All of the following are signs of anorexia nervosa EXCEPT:**
(Average)

A. Malnutrition
B. Behavior regression
C. No outward signs
D. Recognizable weight loss

Answer: C. No outward signs
There are significant outward signs displayed when a person is struggling with anorexia.

137. **Which of the following refers to a muscle's ability to contract over a period of time and maintain strength?**
(Rigorous)

A. Cardiovascular fitness
B. Muscle endurance
C. Muscle fitness
D. Muscle force

Answer: B. Muscle endurance
Cardiovascular fitness relates to the ability to perform moderate-to-high-intensity exercise for a prolonged period. Muscular fitness relates to how much force a muscle group can generate (strength) and how effectively the muscle group can sustain that force over a period of time (endurance).

138. **A game of "Simon Says" is an opportunity for the teacher to asses which of the following:**
(Average)

A. Concept of body awareness
B. Concept of spatial awareness
C. Concept of direction and movement
D. Concept of speed and movement

Answer: A. Concept of body awareness
Instructors can assess body awareness by playing and watching a game of "Simon Says" and asking the students to touch different body parts. You can also instruct students to make their bodies into various shapes, from straight to round to twisted and varying sizes, to fit into different sized spaces.

139. **Bending, stretching, and turning are examples of which type of skill?**
     (*Average*)

     A. Locomotor skills
     B. Nonlocomotor skills
     C. Manipulative skills
     D. Rhythmic skills

Answer: B. Nonlocomotor skills
Locomotor skills move an individual from one point to another. Nonlocomotor skills are stability skills in which the movement requires little or no movement of one's base of support and does not result in change of position. Manipulative skills use body parts to propel or receive objects, controlling them primarily with the hands and feet. Rhythmic skills include responding and moving the body in time with the beat, tempo, or pitch of music.

140. **Which of the following statements is NOT true?**
     (*Rigorous*)

     A. Children's motor development and physical fitness are affected by a range of factors, including social, psychological, familial, genetic, and cultural factors
     B. Motor development is complete by the time a student reaches sixth grade
     C. A family's economic status can affect a student's motor development
     D. A physical education program can have a positive impact on a student's level of physical fitness

Answer: B. Motor development is complete by the time a student reaches sixth grade
Motor development continues until adulthood. Furthermore, many factors have an impact on children's motor development and physical fitness.